CZECH BLUEGRASS

FOLKLORE STUDIES IN A MULTICULTURAL WORLD

The Folklore Studies in a Multicultural World series is a collaborative venture of the University of Illinois Press, the University Press of Mississippi, the University of Wisconsin Press, and the American Folklore Society, made possible by a generous grant from the Andrew W. Mellon Foundation. The series emphasizes the interdisciplinary and international nature of current folklore scholarship, documenting connections between communities and their cultural production. Series volumes highlight aspects of folklore studies such as world folk cultures, folk art and music, foodways, dance, African American and ethnic studies, gender and queer studies, and popular culture.

Czech Bluegrass

NOTES FROM THE HEART OF EUROPE

LEE BIDGOOD

UNIVERSITY OF ILLINOIS PRESS
Urbana, Chicago, and Springfield

Publication of this book is supported in part by grants from the Andrew W. Mellon Foundation and the L. J. and Mary C. Skaggs Folklore Fund.

1 2 3 4 5 C P 5 4 3 2 1
∞ This book is printed on acid-free paper.

Library of Congress Control Number: 2017946000
ISBN 978-0-252-04145-7 (hardcover)
ISBN 978-0-252-08300-6 (paperback)
ISBN 978-0-252-05005-3 (e-book)

CONTENTS

FOREWORD BY TONY TRISCHKA

Sometime in the mid-1980s, I received a photo in the mail from someone in Czechoslovakia. It was a posed picture of some twenty-five (or perhaps more) Czech banjoists at a rural gathering. The idea that that many five-stringers existed in one place at one time in a communist country was surprising, to put it mildly. A few years later, in 1988, I found myself and my Skyline bandmates winging our way on Czech Air to that very country. My about-to-be new friend Robert Braun, a terrific banjoist, had set up a tour of the country that would take us from Plzeň to Bratislava and many points in between. To this day, it stands in my mind and heart as the most moving and rewarding tour I've ever done.

In our travels, we discovered what we already knew—that east or west, capitalist or communist, people are basically the same, with the same concerns, and music is the lingua franca to bridge artificial barriers.

We found ourselves playing our American music to large crowds while oversized hammers and sickles adorned the background near the venues. On our first day there, I was fortunate to meet luthier Jaroslav Průcha, who, in exchange for my letting him spend an hour disassembling my Stelling banjo to take exacting measurements, gave me one of his wonderful instruments. We were also able to share the bill with Poutníci (Pilgrims), a very popular national band with exceedingly talented musicians, including Robert Křesťan, Luboš Malina, and Luboš Novotný. Since Robert and Luboš M. both played banjo, the populace of Czechoslovakia became open to the radical concept that bluegrass and related musics had a right to achieve a wide audience, a situation unheard of in the United States.

As we toured the country, we co-billed with other groups, which allowed us to get a good fix on the varieties of sounds being created on non-Appalachian terrain. Some of the bands, singing in their own languages, hewed to the traditional roots of bluegrass. Others used a general bluegrass structure to create new, more personal sounds. We would be invited into people's homes, where I would find photocopied versions of my banjo instruction books and cassette copies of our albums. Someone would manage to bring one "official" item into the country, and then there'd be a diaspora of the material in question as copies made the rounds of the bluegrass community.

The most memorable moment of the tour for us was our appearance at Porta Fest in Plzeň. We were one of many bands on the bill, and we played our set at night in front of thirty thousand people in an amphitheater normally used to watch walk-in (as opposed to "drive-in") movies. Every third or fourth person in the audience was holding a candle, making for an amazing light-dappled view from the stage. The fact that we sang in English was noteworthy, and at the end of our set we went backstage and were called out for an encore. We did one more tune and went backstage again, only to be retrieved a final time—now, though, being told to leave our instruments behind. At that point, the emcee brought us to the front of the stage. He said, "You've given us the gift of your music. Now we'd like to give you a gift." He then divided the audience into thirds, ten thousand people in each, and, starting with the left side, had each group sing one note of a major triad. Words can't express . . .

I've given you a snapshot of one of the many tours I've done in Czechoslovakia, and then primarily the Czech Republic, to give you my experience of what Lee Bidgood so ably describes in these pages. This is a topic well worthy of detailed exploration! Of the many countries that have caught the bluegrass bug—Japan in the late 1970s and France in the mid-1980s being the most notable after the Czech Republic—the Czech immersion in bluegrass has had the deepest roots and has been the longest lasting. Groups like Druhá Tráva, evolved from Poutníci though by no means strictly bluegrass, have kept the flame blazing, in both Europe and the United States. Jaroslav Průcha now makes banjos for Béla Fleck and Alison Brown, as well as parts for major banjo makers in the States. Zdeněk Roh also makes beautiful banjos, one of which I proudly own. A first-rate Dobro festival (lest we forget, John Dopyera, the inventor of the resophonic guitar, was born in Slovakia) has taken place most years in Slovakia.

Lee Bidgood is the first person to do a serious accounting of the forces, political and artistic, that have contributed to the popularity of this outlier music in this unlikely locale. By putting himself in the narrative, he gives us an up-close and personal sense of the various aspects of the bluegrass and old-time music wave that has swept across the Czech and Slovakian musical landscapes for years—and still counting.

INTRODUCTION

The simple, repeated notes of the shuffle allow a fiddler to set a tempo, call other musicians to order, signal to dancers, and set the tone for the music to come. As a fiddler, I am more used to playing this gesture than talking about it, but as an ethnomusicologist, I am drawn to consider the frame in which the interactive experience of music making starts. In that opening pull of the bow, a fiddler indicates where the tune will lead. Here I lay out a few beats to set the tempo for the rest of this volume.

The personal, embodied nature of my ethnographic fieldwork in the Czech Republic is based in the conviction that my body, my experiences, and my "self" are entwined with those of Czechs like the ones I write about in the text that follows. My account of these relationships is inevitably partial—in two senses. Firstly, the stories in this volume do not provide a comprehensive panorama of Czech bluegrass history, because my fieldwork research has necessarily led me to focus on documenting and participating in certain parts of the contemporary Czech bluegrass world, those where I was invited, and those where I felt comfortable working and playing.

This admission of partiality is also a disclaimer about my narrow field of experience and the lenses through which I sense the world around me. I participated in bluegrass first, as a fiddler and mandolinist, and came to write about the music only later. What's more, though as of this writing I have been working to understand Czech bluegrass music making for sixteen years, this is still my first foray into a book-length study. It reflects the side of the community that I have seen thus far—and that has been revealed to me by my colleagues in the Czech Republic.

Put another way, my account is naïve, again in multiple senses. In the pages that follow, despite my best efforts, I sometimes reveal my lack of experience, wisdom, or judgment. I have tried to keep this account simple in the sense of the term "naïve" as I saw it applied to folk art in Czech museums: a straightforward style that deliberately rejects sophistication in an attempt to communicate directly. This choice is an attempt to reflect what Czech bluegrassers have been toward me: open, hospitable, straightforward, honest. I imagine that there are some things they chose not to tell me, but there is little they tried to hide. I try to be similarly direct and circumspect.

This directness emerges in my focus on stories. Many of the Czech bluegrassers with whom I conducted interviews were eager both to tell their story and to hear mine. Of course, the individuals whom I met more informally—especially those I played music with—were often eager to hear my thoughts on how the Czech scene compared to what I knew about bluegrass in the United States. Before any of this could happen, there had to be a connection established of camaraderie, of some willingness to engage and relate—a good bit of explanation, sometimes a touch of convincing, and often negotiation of cultural barriers.

My work is based in the scholarly discipline of ethnomusicology, refers to many aspects of Czech culture, and is suffused with the sounds, speech, and social dynamics specific to the making of bluegrass music. I imagine that few readers of this book have a sufficient background in these fields to feel within their comfort zone when reading all of the pages that follow. For an orientation to the Czech words and usages that I will use throughout the book, see the explanatory notes on the Czech language and the glossary, which follow the main text. With respect to bluegrass music itself, I cannot provide enough background in this text, but refer readers who want to learn more to Neil Rosenberg's authoritative *Bluegrass: A History* (1985; revised ed. 2005) for an excellent narrative account, and to Thomas Goldsmith's *The Bluegrass Reader* (2004) for a broader array of perspectives.

As to the story that I will tell, I will approach it by offering an introduction of the kind that I typically use in field research. This critical part of fieldwork is where I work to establish rapport and begin a relationship through disclosure—through telling stories about myself. I will then transition to thanking the people who have reciprocated my offering of story by giving me theirs. As with all research of this kind, this book would not exist without the generosity of the many people who prepared me to make the journey from North Carolina to Prague in the first place, those who welcomed me into a world where Czech bluegrass has begun to make sense, and those who have helped me find a path in research and mark it so that readers can make the trip themselves.

INTRODUCING MYSELF

As a child I was drawn into the Suzuki method of teaching and learning musicality by wanting to play the violin like my older sister. After elementary-school participation in the suburban Suzuki method scene, our family moved to a rural corner of north-central Florida. Tired of the commute to lessons and performances in the county seat, my parents asked us kids if we *really* wanted to keep taking music lessons. I was the only one who answered yes, so they asked around about local music teachers and found a local fiddler who offered to teach me. Through lessons with David Fontana and then through playing in his band, I soon was steeped in the technique and repertory of fiddling and the southern American string band.

I began to sense as a ten-year-old that there were different modes of "musical 'being in the world'"—different ways of creating and inhabiting musicalities (Titon 1997, 31). David took me to an old-time jam in Micanopy, Florida, where I encountered teachers and players like Tom Staley and Fay Baird. I remember people jamming in different rooms of the house, dancing, eating, and playing as kids wove in and out of the circles. With the band I traveled to the 1991 Florida Folk Festival at White Springs, where I competed and placed in the junior division of the fiddle contest, and won a check for something in the neighborhood of eleven dollars.[1]

After another move, this time to North Carolina, my sisters and I returned to "classical" training, and my shift to studying the viola allowed me to keep the violin for "fiddling." As I differentiated myself from my structures of origin, I found more avenues to explore in bluegrass and Irish music, attending weekly jams at a pub and traveling to bluegrass festivals. I eventually landed a spot playing fiddle and mandolin in Fescue 911, a band (there "for all your bluegrass emergencies!") of men and women almost my parents' age who were part of our church congregation.

As an undergraduate viola major at the University of North Carolina at Chapel Hill, I kept up with bluegrass, playing mandolin and fiddle with a group of fellow students called the Steep Canyon Rangers. During this same period of time, I was attracted to another musicality within the music department. Music professor Brent Wissick had sensed my affinity for musical exploration and directed me to the field of early music, where I played baroque and renaissance viola and began study of the viola da gamba. Through early

The author on stage with the Steep Canyon Rangers, ca. 1999.

music I began to recognize that there are not only different forms of musicality, but distinct social and professional worlds in which these musicalities are formed. My budding interest in music as culture was also sparked by courses in folklore and American studies that helped focus my interests.

I had gotten wind of bluegrass activity in the Czech Republic in the late 1990s, about the same time that I was considering a study-abroad semester in Prague. My curiosity was piqued by online information about groups like Druhá Tráva and instrument makers such as Rosťa Čapek and Jiří Lebeda that hinted at an extensive Czech bluegrass scene. During my first visit as a study-abroad student in 2000, I saw several public performances by bluegrass bands, visited with instrument makers, met some Prague musicians, and got a chance to see that the community was indeed significant.

After returning to the United States, I kept up my engagement through Czech language courses and music class projects on Czech bluegrass, as I was beginning to learn about ethnomusicology in a course with Sarah Weiss. American studies classes with Bob Cantwell (also a former member of Fescue 911) inspired me to think critically about the ways in which bluegrass plays out in a variety of contexts. He also suggested that I look at the graduate program in music at the University of Virginia, where Michelle Kisliuk connected my interests in bluegrass and ethnomusicology.

My growing interest in the cultural contexts of music led me to apply for a Fulbright Student Grant to study how bluegrass has taken root and grown in the Czech Republic. As a Fulbrighter during 2002–2003, I stumbled into relationships and understandings that remain strong and growing today—with Sunny Side and fiddler Jirka Králík, then with Zdeněk Roh and his circle in the Vysočina highlands east of Prague, and with the Prague circle around the U Supa jam. It was during this fieldwork year that I began speaking and understanding Czech with a degree of fluency.

In the fall of 2003, I returned to the United States and began my PhD studies at the University of Virginia. During each of the next three summers, I returned to the Czech Republic. In 2004 I was invited (and hired, in the sense that my airfare was provided) to play with Zdeněk Roh's band "Roll's Boys" at a festival in Norway. The following year found me with a grant to study the Czech language in Brno (the Czech Republic's second city, next in size to Prague and located southeast of the capital city) and time to tour with Roll's Boys on the side.

In 2006 I again traveled with Roll's Boys to play, this time a festival in Denmark and some gigs in the Czech Republic. That fall I hosted a visiting Czech bluegrasser in Virginia, and enjoyed introducing him to the American South. For the school year of 2007–2008 I was in Prague again, for another

The author with Roll's Boys at the Banjo Jamboree festival in Čáslav, Czech Republic, 2008.

The author on stage with Peter O. Ruby and All Bells and Whistles at the European World of Bluegrass festival in La Roche-sur-Foron, France, 2007.

research stay, falling into now-familiar patterns working with Roll's Boys, as well as more involvement in the circle around the band Reliéf and with Petr Hrubý (aka Peter O. Ruby), and also Prague's academic ethnomusicology community.

In 2009 I squeezed in a short visit during the summer, performing, teaching, and conducting several interviews. After beginning my career as an academic faculty member in 2010, I continued my fieldwork, with visits in 2011 to shoot a documentary film about the Czech bluegrass scene and in 2013 to show a preliminary version of the film to Czech audiences for feedback. The resulting film (*Banjo Romantika*, dir. Shara Lange, 2015) dominated my field research, both as a means for opening conversations and because I did a lot of work to collect material and permissions for the project.

GRATITUDE

I have been working on parts of this text since 2007. While many of my Czech bluegrass colleagues were intrigued by *Banjo Romantika*, few have been excited about this process, as an academic book lies far outside their realms of experience or interest. Many Czech bluegrassers have told me that they are glad I am telling their story, however—they want *you* to read all this! I am grateful for their willingness to spend time with me, for their explanations, and for their enthusiasm.

This book is about Czech bluegrass, but it also includes the story about how I discovered it, how I have come to understand it, and how I see it fitting into the larger worlds of music and society. I focus most on relationships, perceptions, and meaning—what I call the pragmatics of musical practice. Like my Czech bluegrass colleagues, I believe that making music is a necessary part of life; I have learned from them how to structure my life so that music can flourish in it. With their help, I have found ways to work and play through an ostensibly foreign and improbable musical phenomenon.

I thank first the people who agreed to join me as characters in the story I tell. Zdeněk, Zdeňka, the Fischers and all of the Kamarádi balkánského rance and Luka nad Jihlavou communities, Zbyněk Bureš, Tomáš Dvořák, Jirka Králík, and many more Czech bluegrassers taught me that work can blend with play and lead to lasting friendships. You all have fed me, taught me, housed me, transported me, and welcomed me into your lives. I am honored to be known as *strejda* (uncle) by your kids, and hope I can live up to that title as part of the bluegrass family. The Tuesday and Thursday night jamming crews at U Supa now are dispersed, but I hold on to memories from our circles, and to this day I try to follow Věra's instructions on how (*not*) to pour beer.

The Fulbright Commission in Prague has continued to support my work since I held a student grant in 2002–2003. Irena Přibylová and Zuzana Jurková have continued to help me understand how my project fits into the literature and practice of Czech academia. Thanks as well to Ted and all the Turnaus and to Melinda Reidinger for their thoughtful conversations about Czech culture and just about everything.

My thanks to Sarah Weiss, Brent Wissick, Bob Cantwell, Jocelyn Neal, and others at and around the University of North Carolina at Chapel Hill who helped point me in a number of useful directions and continue to inspire me. Thanks as well to the Steep Canyon Rangers for a taste of the working life in a bluegrass band—and for helping me make the decision to go to graduate school; and to Fescue 911, John Templeton, Michael Stam, Joseph DeCosimo, and other Tar Heels who remain friends and musical coconspirators. The Carrboro folks who encouraged me in writing are many: Vimala, Rush, Charles Pettee, the Compound, and all y'all.

I am deeply indebted to the folks at the University of Virginia who helped me form this project's foundations and carry it through graduate school and beyond. Michelle Kisliuk's passion and vision and Richard Will's calm lucidity kept me fueled and centered during my years as a grad student. The bluegrass jam, Collegium, and Consort on Campus, as well as old-time tunes with Ben, Aaron, and Mary Jane, provided a soundtrack as my work developed. Mary Simonson and Shana Goldin-Perschbacher were my neighbors in the music library and continue to serve as my academic big sisters; Alli, Michael, Loren, Nick, Dave, and all the musgrads helped me learn that our research happens best in community.

My thanks to Jon Dueck, Jeff Titon, and others who read through and provided useful feedback on parts of this manuscript as it neared completion. I am grateful for the detailed comments and large-scale suggestions from the scholars who read through the whole thing: Irena Přibylová, Neil Rosenberg, Erika Brady, and Fred Bartenstein. Thanks as well to Jane Lyle, whose expert copyediting and familiarity with Czech bluegrass fine-tuned this volume from stem to stern. I am humbled by the support I have received from the University of Illinois Press. The Folklore Studies in a Multicultural World workshop and Laurie Matheson's encouragement for this project have been critical in turning this text into a book. This press is continuing Judith McCulloh's courageous vision for including books on bluegrass as part of the scholarly literature.

I am grateful for the support for this project that I have received from my colleagues at East Tennessee State University in the Department of Appalachian Studies and Bluegrass, Old Time, and Country Music Studies. This book is more readable and engaging because of the time I have spent with faculty and students here. I am both blessed and challenged as I write about Czech bluegrass sitting in an office in northeast Tennessee, a place that Tim Stafford (1987) once called the "cradle of bluegrass." I am grateful for the Nashville-based International Country Music Conference community who have made me feel part of a cohort of scholars who love the music they study. This volume's consideration of place is more focused thanks to the field of Appalachian studies and its critical regionalist perspective on the interactions of the local and the global.

I dedicate this work to the people who have taught me to love and be loved, to speak, listen, and hear. To my mother, who taught me to read and to love reading, and to my father, who provided me a model for working as a researcher and as an author. Last of all to Emily, whose clear-headed fierceness keeps me grounded, and who is my favorite singing, reading, and writing partner. I am so thankful.

CZECH BLUEGRASS

Map of the Czech Republic.

1

PLACE, MEANING, COMMUNITY, AND IN-BETWEENNESS

RELIÉF AND PERFORMING IN BETWEEN

In May 2003 I was most of the way through my first year of fieldwork, living in the Czech Republic and seeking connections with musicians and other participants in bluegrass music. A contact I had recently made with banjoist and luthier Zdeněk Roh led me to the village of Lhotka u Telče, where I took part in a weekend *dílna* (workshop) along with dozens of students who were learning bluegrass repertory and style. The setting was Kozlova Stodola (Goat's Barn), a small, unofficial *pension* where I was lodged and fed along with a few dozen other students on the edge of a wood in the Czecho-Moravian highlands two hours' drive southeast of Prague, the Czech capital. The teachers were the members of Reliéf, a Prague bluegrass group known on the Czech scene for their skilled picking and soulful vocal harmonies.

The students were divided into classes by instrument: bassists, guitarists, banjoists, and mandolinists. Each group would work separately during the morning and afternoon sessions, with some special sessions at which all the students would gather. During the "band workshop" session, students gathered to sit on the ground in front of an impromptu stage area set up outside the community/dining room, with a PA system assembled from well-worn and mismatched sound equipment. As part of the mandolin group, I blended in, setting up my MiniDisc recorder alongside other students who wanted to capture the insights that the band of teachers would provide.

The members of Reliéf show students how to use a microphone in live performance, Lhotka u Telče, 2003.

Grouped as if they were on stage, the members of Reliéf addressed a number of practical concerns: how to use microphones, how to arrange the vocals for *a cappella* gospel songs, how to accompany singing with background instruments, and other techniques common to bluegrass music performance. In the following excerpt from this session, Tomáš Dvořák, the mandolin player, raises a point of standard bluegrass performance practice. Guitarist Jirka Holoubek joins in, and banjoist Zbyněk Bureš jokingly complicates things at the end:

TD: I'd like to add something about solos. I told the mandolinists, and it applies generally. I don't think it's come up so far. Since the majority of songs start with some kind of solo—for instance, the banjo . . . as with "Blue Ridge Cabin Home" when we play it. So, the first solo simply must be melodic. It must be the . . . like the main melody of the song. It must be clear . . .

JH: . . . it must simply tell the listener what he is to hear.

TD: Exactly—so you can recognize whether it's "Blue Ridge Cabin Home" and not "Page of Memory" [Stránka pamětí] or, I don't know, some other similar song. If you only recognize it by the text, then it's too late. And then . . .

ZB: [interrupting] . . . but when you play "Sweetheart You Done Me Wrong" and "Stránka pamětí," you can only tell them apart by the text.

TD: One is English, one is Czech.

ZB: One is English, one is Czech—though they're altogether different songs, the motif is the same.

JH: But that's Petr Kůs's problem. [laughing]

ZB: It's Bill Monroe's problem, because he was inspired by Petr Kůs.[1]

Much of the bluegrass-related music played in the Czech Republic is directly lifted from US practice and repertory, and as Zbyněk points out, a sizable number of these pieces have corresponding Czech texts or are reproduced in songs with a considerable overlap of "motif" or melodic/harmonic/rhythmic/textual elements. The text of the Monroe song "Sweetheart You Done Me Wrong" (Flatt and Monroe, BMI, 1948) is widely known in bluegrass circles, and the song by Kůs is available on his website. I include here my translation of "Stránka pamětí" to provide a sense of Kůs's poetry:

Stránka pamětí (by Petr Kůs)

I wipe the nostalgia from my eyes
when I think back on my youth.
Street-corner loves I used to have,
a children's book all full of lies.

My path has a far-off goal.
I can recall how I've lived here.
I can hardly hide the tears
on the page of these memories.[2]

The two songs do share a similar melody (if not the same one), so Zbyněk's interjection makes sense. But outside of the specific situation Tomáš describes, this doesn't seem like too much of a problem: both songs circulate in the Czech bluegrass scene, and are "kicked off" with any number of instrumental introductions.

What exactly is the issue here? Is it a "problem" that Petr Kůs used a well-known bluegrass song as the chassis for his own poetic Czech text? Jirka seems to suggest that this is the case: that the problem is one of appropriation—a concern that remains relevant in considering popular music of all sorts. The laughter that spread through the audience at the end of the exchange I quote above indicates how this problem helps define Czech bluegrass, however. Zbyněk turns this problem on its ear, showing that it is also an opportunity. He jokes that it was Kůs who actually inspired Monroe, a joke that would make sense only in Czech—not just in the Czech language, but in the sort of particularly Czech bluegrass scene such as the workshop environment. This context opens a space for the unlikely situation in which Kůs would be well enough known to be compared—even in a joke—to the "Father of Bluegrass," Bill Monroe. In this kind of space, Czech bluegrassers remake this music to fit their world; in creating this kind of space, they make their world fit this music.

Czechs can claim some actual, if tenuous, influences on American bluegrass culture. If they acknowledge their historic link with Slovaks, Czechs can own a connection to the Dobro, a steel-string guitar (sometimes called a resophonic guitar) developed in the 1920s by John Dopyera and his brothers Emil and Rudy, Slovakia-born luthiers who were working in the United States. The instrument's name is a bit of wordplay: it is drawn from the phrase "DOpyera BROthers," but the resulting word also means "good" in both the Slovak and Czech languages.

Buck "Josh" Graves connected the Dobro with bluegrass through his influential work with Flatt and Scruggs. Czechs can thus find a bit of real history to spin into a rationale—if they feel that they need one—for their participation in bluegrass, an ostensibly foreign music. Elsewhere (Bidgood, forthcoming) I have used Ruth Ellen Gruber's (2009) term "real imaginary" to characterize the sense of place that Czech bluegrassers create through songwriting. In emphasizing the idea of "in-betweenness" here, I allow for both real connections between Czechs and bluegrass (like that to the Dopyeras) and those, like Zbyněk's joke, that are more playful. Anthropologist David Samuels (2005) has noted the importance of humor and play as part of not only the mechanism of negotiating the contradictions of meaning in contemporary culture, but also the way we should study culture. With him, I strive for an analysis of meaning "that admits the ambiguous nature of the pointing gesture," viewing the relationship between culture and expression as one that "takes on the nature of a pun—the structure of a sign that points in multiple directions at once" (6, 8). Kristin Solli (2006, 9) has identified this kind of multiplicity in her study of Norwegian country music, observing that American cultural elements can sometimes lead to ambiguous or contradictory meanings: "in Norway a cowboy hat points to a borrowed cultural tradition and a local history and tradition. As such it is 'foreign' and simultaneously intimately familiar, and never stops pointing in both directions at the same time."

Many of the people about whom I write in this volume were in earshot of Zbyněk's joke in 2003. My growing cultural fluency over the years since I recorded it has allowed me more insights into their nuanced senses of humor, senses that often fit with Svetlana Boym's (2001, xviii) characterization of "reflective nostalgia." Boym's term evokes an "ironic and humorous" affective state in which "longing and critical thinking are not opposed to one another" (49–50), a description that resonates with my observations of the ways that Czechs have joined bluegrass songs and sounds with their

European environments. Zbyněk's quip reflects this kind of self-conscious longing for places that never were—what Boym calls "a romance with one's own fantasy" (xiii), in which participants are aware of the fictions involved in their earnest activity .

When I first heard about Czechs who sang and played bluegrass, I was initially curious, wondering how they performed an American music style. However, moments like the one I describe above first attracted my attention to Czech bluegrass-related music making not simply as an extension of the global "diaspora" of bluegrass, but as a form of revival and transformation that can best be understood on its own terms. Reliéf and their audience build traditions that lie between strict identifications as Czech or American, and they also discuss them self-consciously—and laugh about the things that don't always fit. Czech re-creations of bluegrass music lead to situations like the liminal moment that Zbyněk describes, a potentially awkward moment in which a listener won't know what song will be introduced, what language will emerge from a singer's lips, and what musical canons will be invoked.

While performances and receptions of bluegrass music (including my work) happen between people, they are also informed by media and other forms of interaction, and are shaped by negotiations of space and place where that "betweenness" gains heightened importance. I describe my experiences with Czech bluegrassers and explain their music making in part as a negation or subversion of existing cultural, political, and economic structures ("Is this music American or Czech?"), but also as an earnestly playful negotiation of self and other, now and then, here and there.[3] In their performances of Americanness and bluegrass, Czechs can critique or even disrupt their own social or geographic situation; sometimes (or at the same time) they can reinforce their own Czechness and Europeanness. As I have learned, identity, community, and history form a complicated set of dynamics in the postsocialist Czech Republic—both for Czechs and for a visitor like me.

It is the centrality of relationship itself, and the discourse that arises from human relations, that I consider to constitute the basis for Czech bluegrass music making. Bluegrassers carry out their musical projects in large part through negotiation with colleagues, peers, friends, and others around them. Jokes are told and understood, lessons are learned and ignored, and musical vibrations themselves have real presence *between* people.

I have adopted the idea of "in-betweenness" as a way of describing how Czech bluegrass music makers situate themselves in relation to "America," and as a way of considering their project as a whole. Czech bluegrassers, like the members of Reliéf, draw from and perform both Czech and American elements to create something that is "in between": uniquely linked to both, but distinct from either. Furthermore, the process of my work is informed by James Clifford's (1986, 2–3) description of ethnography as "actively situated *between* powerful systems of meaning. It poses its questions at the boundaries of civilizations, cultures, classes, races, and genders." Lastly, in a concrete way, the categories of "Czech" and "American" and all that lies between them are part of performances of and reactions to bluegrass music that happen *between* people, as a part of media and other forms of communication within and between places.

PLACE AND AUTHENTICITY

Bluegrass is one of many rural-based music practices that are linked to particular places (both real and imagined) in the United States. Aaron Fox (2004) connects in nuanced ways the music and community making in his study of country music in a specific part of Texas. Few studies of country music, however, are as limited and precise in the claims that they make between people, place, and music.

Scholars and industry stakeholders have their own reasons for emphasizing—using much broader brushstrokes—an exclusive relationship between "country" musics and certain parts of the American South. In his critique of Bill Malone's "southern thesis" for the genesis of country music, folklorist Clifford Murphy (2014, 21–22) argues that industry stakeholders and scholars have propagated a "myth of southern authenticity" in music—one that doesn't stand up to the variety of country music scenes and practices that exist across the US and Canada, as well as overseas. Keith Negus (1999, 103–130) illustrates how rhetoric based in "family, community and the common people" (130) continues to give the contemporary Nashville country music industry a distinctly "southern" accent—one that is eminently marketable. As an acoustic and more rustic-seeming form of country music, bluegrass is often considered an exemplar of southern American music, especially in earlier scholarship: Robert Cantwell (1984) called it "the Old Southern sound," building on Mayne Smith's (1965, 245) foundational description of bluegrass (in an academic paper that was one of the first to consider the genre) as music "played by . . . Southern musicians, primarily for a Southern audience [and] stylistically based on Southern musical traditions."

Czech bluegrass- and country-related projects could be considered as somehow less "real," lacking proximity to or cultural fluency with the geographic and cultural milieus from which country music's early stars emerged, or the media that bring country music to the wider world. The existing literature on bluegrass music and geography is largely built on work by George

Carney (1998, 148–150; 1974, 35–40), who has mapped birthplaces of musicians and the diffusion of some bluegrass-related cultural productions without questioning the ways in which these ideas emerge as part of change and movement, especially in light of the deterritorializing processes of media like radio and records. In identifying certain parts of piedmont and western North Carolina as the culture hearth for bluegrass, Carney's work treats the music as a fixed and permanently rooted phenomenon. More recent geographic work shows that it is possible to consider social and political pressures and changes (Mitchell 2000) and provide more nuanced treatment of the paradoxes of stasis and change in natural, built, and cultural spaces and places (Massey 1994, 2005).

Carney's focus on a static location as a place of origin for bluegrass is odd, as the history of bluegrass performers, media, and fandom has always been dynamic. Movement, change, and adaptation are some of the most abiding constants in the history of bluegrass, starting with the early career of Bill Monroe and his brothers in Chicago—where they had traveled in the 1930s in search of jobs they could not obtain in their home region of western Kentucky (Rosenberg 2005, 29). In describing the Monroe brothers' migrations in search of work in the early professional "hillbilly" music industry, Rosenberg indicates how musicians' traveling life added additional and more complicated patterns of migration to those of the Hillbilly Highway that led many Appalachian residents north in the first half of the twentieth century (Guy 2007). From the radio "barnstorming" days of early bluegrass-type bands through the globalizing spread of the music that followed the postwar folk revival, aesthetic, political, cultural, and technological changes have transformed how people make, use, and think about bluegrass music.

My study can be read as an argument that the meaning and utility of bluegrass-related activities only increase as they take place in more—and more diverse—locales. Considering the in-between activities of Czech bluegrass, I add to the growing body of work that provides alternatives to the essentializing narratives of heritage and place identity that have accrued to bluegrass in its relatively short history, as well as country music at large. I follow Sweet (1996) in questioning how bluegrass-related music making affects lived reality beyond Appalachia—looking as well at other places where country musics like bluegrass are cultivated. Scott Hambly (1980) pioneered the study of what he called "extracontextual bluegrass" with his examination of the intersections of the music with the culture of the San Francisco Bay area. Rosenberg's (2005, 369–374) "Bibliographical Notes" at the end of his *Bluegrass: A History* point to many of these scenes, and studies in the decades since show that the contexts where bluegrass can thrive are many and diverse. Finch's (2016) study of the Toronto Area Bluegrass Committee offers insight into scenes that formed around this music in Canada, with a particular focus on bluegrass's inroads into urban milieus during and after the folk revival of the 1960s. Gardner's (2004) study of festival culture in the "Rocky Mountain Bluegrass Scene" illustrates the ways in which fans create distinct and thriving social structures through this music, far from the working-class and rural environs of the eastern United States. Haslam, Haslam Russell, and Chon (1999) show that working-class country music culture thrives even in California; Solli's (2006) study of country music as an integrated part of Norwegian culture and politics, Samuels's (2005) volume on country as a part of life on the San Carlos Apache Reservation, and Dent's (2009) study of "hick" elements of *música sertaneja* in Brazil are yet more examples of productive reterritorializations of bluegrass and country sounds, practices, and tropes (Deleuze and Guattari 2002, 10).[4]

Ideas about authenticity are key to place identities in bluegrass practice, as Bealle (1993) shows in his study of how bands introduce and talk about themselves on stage at a bluegrass festival. Place is also central to bluegrass scholarship, as Carney's works and Cherre's (2013) reliance on Appalachian linguistic traits indicate. Many insider and outsider descriptions of bluegrass music characterize it as an intensely "real" form of country music, due to its acoustic sound, its rural origin stories, and the small-scale nature of bluegrass industries. Scholars are more reserved about this characterization but acknowledge the existence of the perception, for example, stating that bluegrass has attracted fans "with a traditional bent" (Malone and Neal 2010, 323). Richard Peterson (1997, 150–155) discusses the role bluegrass served within the country music industry as a venue for a "hard-core" expression of traditionalism.

At the same time, Peterson (1997, 207–209) also maintains that authenticities in country music are fabricated as part of a renewable industrial system that hinges on audience imagination and artist creativity. He identifies a variety of ways in which artists, fans, and other stakeholders in country music making assert claims of "realness." Some of them can be inherently contradictory; for example, his concept of the authenticity of a "relic, not changed" that might be attributed to the vocal performance of Ralph Stanley is entirely different from the authenticity that he labels "real, not imitative," or that which he terms "credible in current context," labels that could apply to performances by contemporary artists whose approach differs vastly from Stanley's but who have a similar rhetorical effect and affective power.

The very word "scene," which I use above to describe examples of bluegrass activity, is a term that can serve to either undermine or reinforce a sense of identify or coherence.[5] Bennett and Peterson's (2004) volume outlines a framework for considering contemporary scenes, including the ideas of local, virtual, and translocal networks of music practice that I use in this volume. As they make music within local and global frames, Czech bluegrassers adopt and reshape bluegrass for their own place, time, and purposes. Inhabiting and reinforcing their scene within the larger bluegrass world, they decide not only what they do with the music, but how they approach it, how they explain their use of it, and how they worry and argue about the whole process.

BLUEGRASS AND GENRE: ARTICULATING THE COMMUNITY

As they use the term "bluegrass," Czechs reach far from their Central European location to the rolling horse-country hills of Kentucky, to the Grand Ole Opry in Nashville, Tennessee, and to other far-off places. Even in the United States—where the gesture toward the rural and ideal world of bluegrass doesn't require as long a stretch—bluegrass is not an easy thing to pin down. Bluegrass was born out of large-scale contestation, conflict, and social change in the mid-twentieth century, but it remains a way of making music that reflects on a number of rural and urban locales, on stars and other luminaries, and on the everyday people whose lives are part of creating the music, and thus are key to what I call *being* bluegrass.

Taking part in bluegrass music making—being a bluegrasser—can mean many things, from professional work as a performer, to weekly jam attendance with friends, to running a small business producing banjo bridges. Bluegrass participants' almost religious devotion to the music and their attention to musical sounds and their history have made this genre especially prone to simplification into a set of techniques and sounds that refer to the past, often to a canonical set of sound recordings. In practice, however, bluegrass is so much more. I regard bluegrass not as a fixed form or set of sounds, but as a process through which people enact the structures of the music in their particular time, place, and social setting. The sonic and social results of this process of emplacement are what has made bluegrass so engaging, adaptable, and durable. This process-oriented view is what causes me to classify bluegrass as part of the "folk" phenomenon, in particular as a continuation of the folk revival of the latter half of the 1900s. While some parts of bluegrass may derive from a particular folkloric regional tradition, the music-making process as a whole includes processes of transmission, celebration, and curation that fit with many definitions of "folk."

My conception of bluegrass as a "folk" process is in tension with its competing role as a popular music. The early history of bluegrass shows that it was clearly a tool used by artists to gain a foothold in the popular music industry. It has experienced periods of mainstream success, and remains a marginal part of the larger formations of popular culture: as a highly specific subgenre of country music, as a commercial product, and as a lifestyle label detached from any specific musical form. There *is* a "mainstream" to bluegrass, with its trade and fan associations, its awards shows, and its halls of fame.[6] There are industries such as record companies, instrument and accessory suppliers, and publishers associated with bluegrass. But this "mainstream" is itself marginal to the actual mainstream of *more* popular music, and the small scale of these industries serves only to underline the marginal nature of bluegrass.

Some American bluegrassers might fear that the Grammy Award for "Best Bluegrass Album" and the International Bluegrass Music Association's activities homogenize and professionalize bluegrass too much, since these institutions promote the commercial elements and not the community-based aspects of the music. Countering the somewhat paranoid fear of "pseudo-individualization" through consumption of manufactured musical material,[7] I view bluegrass as a form of popular culture that continues to flourish because of its characteristic modes of "active consumption."[8]

Still, this flourishing happens on a small scale. US Bluegrass is a "small" music[9]—and Czech bluegrass represents a small outpost of participation in this music. Czechs often experience a heightened sense of marginality as geographic and cultural outsiders approaching bluegrass music—but at the same time experience an intimate connection, as they are members of an intense and densely connected fellowship who seek knowledge and experience together. This intimacy underscores bluegrass's reputation as "picker's music" in which participatory music making is central (Turino 2008, 25–26). There is a great deal of overt participation in the bluegrass traditions of performance and reception across stages, around jam circles, in parking lot picking, in luthiers' workshops, in small businesses, and on radio, television, and the internet. That participants call themselves "bluegrassers" itself reveals a sophisticated understanding of music making as a community effort—they aren't just musicians, they are socially connected participants in a movement in which personal connections constitute "bluegrass" itself.

A concern with ethics is always present in my work, as I am not focusing just on musical sound, but on social relations in music—or rather, music as social relation. Thus I adopt Rockwell's (2007) focus on the relationships that bluegrass sounds and meanings entail, the interpersonal connections that are embodied in music. In this turn from sound to interactions, I focus on intent and the desires of participants in a music-making situation. This is what I identify as the pragmatics of music making in general: the contexts that motivate people and that inform their production and consumption of music. The pragmatics of Czech bluegrass thus encompasses the pleasure of accomplishing a shared goal as well as the conflict that often arises from differing opinions on if and how that goal is reached.

HOW I GOT IN

During my first visit to the Czech Republic in 2000 as a study-abroad student, the band Reliéf was hosting a monthly bluegrass night at the downtown Prague club Malostranská Beseda. The "Czech" side of the show was carried mainly by guitarist Jirka Holoubek, whose Czech-language emcee work artfully filled the spaces between the skillfully performed English-language songs. Jirka's playful banter and engaging stories framed the bluegrass sounds with locally resonant ideas and phrases.

I tried to speak with the members of Reliéf after the show. Based on their flat response to my questions, I thought they seemed uninterested in talking with me—a curious American with little to offer but a few malformed Czech phrases. They had an auditorium full of rapt Czech fans hanging on every word of their American-style singing and their Czech stage presence. I later learned that the members I had spoken with were embarrassed about their lack of English language knowledge!

I found myself in their shoes when I returned to Prague in 2002. I was eager to meet and learn from Czech bluegrassers, but I didn't know how to approach them. I followed up on some scholarly contacts and went to concerts, but I wasn't finding my way inside the scene. I had read a lot of fieldwork guides that mentioned participant observation, but I wasn't sure how to start my participation.

Working on my Czech skills in an intensive Charles University program during the week, on weekends I attended concerts and festivals that I found through online listings and printed information. I attended the Jamgrass

Ticket from Jamgrass festival, Jindřichův Hradec, Czech Republic, 2002. The price of 100 Czech crowns was the equivalent of roughly US $4 at the time.

Schedule for performances during February 2003 at the Malostranská Beseda in Prague, Czech Republic.

festival in South Bohemia, and continued to see Reliéf in their monthly concerts at the Malostranská Beseda, but I was having trouble connecting with people in these scenes.

One evening in late 2002, I attended a concert at CI-5, a working-class "American country" club then located across from the train station in the industrial Prague suburb of Smíchov. I recognized Ivo Drbohlav, a physicist and musician I had met at the Beseda in 2000. He enthusiastically welcomed me to his table, and that's where it all started.

One night during the early spring of 2003, I finally got up the courage to bring my fiddle to a weekly jam session Ivo had invited me to visit. He had described how to get to the Saloon u Supa ("At the Vulture") via Prague's public transportation system: "Take the number 9 tram to the Bertramka stop, walk back toward the city center until you get to the street Na Čečeličce—go up the hill and it's on the right." As I turned from the park surrounding Bertramka (where W. A. Mozart stayed while visiting Prague) and started up that hill with my fiddle in tow, I found myself in the grittiest part of Prague I had yet visited. The coal smoke was stronger here than in the garden suburb of Střešovice, where I had been lucky enough to find a reasonably priced basement apartment earlier that year.[10] Trash littered the streets and the stoop outside the pub halfway up the hill.

I paused at the threshold seeking a hint of what was going on. The clinking of glasses, the whiffs of smoke, and the inebriated shouts reminded me of the late-night rowdiness I had tired of while playing bar gigs with the fledgling band Steep Canyon Rangers in the still-smoky college bars of Chapel Hill, North Carolina, during the late 1990s. There was no way around it, though—I wanted to get involved! So I pushed through the louvered swinging Wild West saloon doors and entered the fray.

The exterior of U Supa, 2016.

The group of men who were seated around a table littered with beer glasses were excited when they saw my violin case, but they were not sure what to make of my broken Czech. They eventually made room; I sat down, but I wasn't sure exactly what to do next. When the next song started, my anxiety over how I would ever start playing disappeared. I heard the familiar chord progression that marks the introduction to the song "Old Home Place," well known among bluegrassers since the Dillards first circulated it in the early 1960s and J. D. Crowe's New South band retooled it in the 1970s.

Although entirely new to the scene and etiquette around me, I immediately could participate more fluidly as a fiddler. The group played many of the songs that I had learned playing in bluegrass circles in Florida, North Carolina, and Virginia, all of which had been retexted—set to new texts in the Czech language. Along with Czech lyrics set to the tunes of classic songs like "Jesse James" and "Blue Ridge Cabin Home," I recognized with some surprise a Czech-texted version of "Sloop John B." Even the songs that I didn't recognize (some of which I later realized were original Czech pieces with no English-language equivalent) were intelligible, as they used the same kinds of chord progressions and performance framings (such as cues for instrumental breaks, intros and endings, and indications of keys) common to most bluegrass jams. Though we were divided by language—my Czech was still developing at that point—we communicated through the shared bluegrass system.[11] The flow that I joined around the table that night became my focus for that year.

From experiences with bluegrass in North Carolina, I already had a sense that the circle of the jam is at the heart of sound and social interactions in bluegrass music making. The jam affords participants a space for singing, playing tunes, competing, and showing off a new instrument, a space for seeking reassurance, community, a spotlight, or just a place to blend in with a crowd. Through jamming, bluegrassers fulfill their individual desires and at the same time become part of a musical and social community by sharing the "special kind of courtesy" that can ease or obstruct musical and social togetherness (Kisliuk 1988).

I grew up with group lessons and concerts that were the epitome of structure and discipline, with prescribed motions, interactions, and sounds. At the age of ten, though, I was introduced to other music-social structures. Thanks to connections that my parents made in the small town where we lived, I started attending old-time string band jams in the surrounding area of north-central Florida in the early 1990s. In contrast to my lessons, these jams were more flexible, determined by participants in the moment, not programmed in advance. They were also less detached from normal life. In contrast to what I sensed as an erasure of the self during a stage performance, a jam seemed a place where you could include elements of your social and aesthetic background as part of the experience.

One element of jams that I perceived as a parallel with the Suzuki system, though, was the structuring role of repertory. As I grew as a musician, I noted that the jams I attended over time were defined by the songs and tunes that participants regularly performed. While the individual elements of a jam and the individual bits of music performed are never exactly the same, patterns always emerge. Though the mix of place, people, and equipment is different for each jam, the particular nature of many bluegrass jams can, over time, come to define and structure them.

Dynamics in jams can tie into larger social tendencies. For example, a form of Czech shyness (which can seem like standoffishness) that I perceived in my early meetings with musicians plays out in jams as well. Many Czechs jam with long-standing playing companions, and only seldom mix with the wider world of players. The close circle of friends and musical collaborators remains reassuringly defined, with a modicum of flexibility to generate new and (re)engaging possibilities for participants. In this way, bluegrass jams serve as bubbles of civil society, as stabilized versions of social life in which musical relations play out idealized social relations with controlled access to the outside.[12]

CONFLICT AND *VONO*

While the Czech bluegrass community features many thriving and harmonious jam circles, it is also composed of individuals and microcommunities that always seem to be butting heads over something. Bluegrass history provides many precedents for this friction. In his song "Cross-Eyed Child," John Hartford (1999) recalls Bill Monroe as fiercely competitive in his early years, pulling out boxing gloves and proposing a fight to round out a day of contentious rehearsal with his band. Hardwig (2001) proposes that Monroe structured bluegrass as a form of male leisure in the American South that shared many aspects with competitive pursuits like cockfighting, horse racing, and baseball. To this day, jam circles can easily turn into (figurative) boxing rings if the social tide turns from cooperation to competition.

Bluegrass still offers many ways and reasons to butt heads—in the United States as well as the Czech Republic. This thread (or perhaps more of a river) of contention has its benefits, however. Since Lester Flatt and Earl Scruggs left Bill Monroe's band in the late 1940s, musicians have frequently left a side-person position in a band to go off on their own, carrying musical ideas from their apprenticeship in the former band, and sometimes some serious grudges (as was the case with Flatt, Scruggs, and Monroe). Band members seem to rotate in and out of Czech bluegrass bands about as fast as they do in the United States. Some top-level bands maintain more stability, but the mid-level semiprofessional bands seem to constantly turn over their membership.

Discontent and the desire to move on from a musical partnership (whether formal or informal) can arise for many reasons. In my Czech fieldwork, I have heard reports of fellow bluegrassers who mess up their breaks, don't show up for rehearsal, don't return borrowed lutherie tools, and even steal instruments. But what about when a jam is under way, and something happens that is an instance not of a legal misstep, but rather of an aesthetic one? In my consideration of pragmatics in musical interactions, I seek examples of understanding, but also cases of misunderstanding. In language, a misunderstanding can result from a grammar problem, a typographical error, or a differing regional dialect or idiom. A misunderstanding might also arise because of context, and from differences in the participants' intent—and these are tied more to relational issues than to a language problem.

Understanding can arise between people in conditions of "intersubjective mutuality . . . shared knowledge, mutual trust, and accord" (Habermas 1979, 32). Czech bluegrassers, being people like the rest of us, do not always live up to these ideals. I have observed and been a part of personal differences and diverging constellations of media-informed ideologies about the music, as well as competing aesthetic and business ideas.

At the beginning of my 2007–2008 research year, I met luthier and mandolinist Eduard "Eda" Krištůfek. During a car ride to a rehearsal, I told Eda that my research areas included fiddling, gospel music, and banjo making. In response, he gave examples of people or situations that fit with my ideas, and then stopped to remark that nearly all of these stories turn out to be instances of estrangement, irritation, or a similar dispute. After some moments of silence while he drove, Eda reflected, hoping that my writing would not turn out to be just a critique of the community, a recounting of bickering and backbiting among Czech bluegrassers.

Eda might be right, as I have turned a critical eye to contentious areas, but not to denigrate or belittle them. Seeking out the unresolved negotiations of Czech bluegrass allows me to focus on what is at stake, what participants value, and how they can forge aesthetic, economic, and ethical compromises. What do Czech bluegrassers see as flexible (what can be adapted to become "bluegrass" or "American"), and what is immutably "Czech" or "American" and cannot be changed? What areas of in-betweenness exist that lead to jokes like the one Zbyněk Bureš made about Bill Monroe and Petr Kůs?

I am not identifying good or bad translations of bluegrass into Czech; rather, I examine struggles with the negotiation of these boundaries as people work in concrete ways with words, sounds, and musical technology. Like my Czech colleagues, I am seeking ways that bluegrass can take root in European soil—it has been growing there for a while, and its existence in the cultural ecosystem by now is a foregone conclusion. The extremes of identification as "Czech" or "American" are thus expressions of intent that allow me to start tracing the contours and trajectories of value and motivation. The negotiation between categories often consists of in-between moments, spaces, and sounds where the exciting process of communication and understanding happens. These are concerns of pragmatics: What are the intents and purposes for which the practices of bluegrass music making provide a vocabulary? How does bluegrass afford Czechs ways of creating music and relationships? What is the shared musical goal that these social formations would move toward?

For years I had heard Czech bluegrassers talking about their goals and preferences using the equivalent of the word "it," and I wondered what "it" they were talking about. This "it" was a particular something known as *ono*. In terms of linguistic gender classes, *ono* is the neuter form of "it," one of the three second person singular pronouns in Czech, along with *on*, the masculine "he," and *ona*, the feminine "she." Unlike normal, everyday pronouns, the "it" that I was hearing about was usually set apart by the addition of the emphatic prefix *v*- (*vono*), which serves as a way of heightening or colloquializing a word that begins with the vowel sound *o*.

Charles Townsend calls this usage one of the most important phonetic features of Czech vernacular, and the most difficult to analyze. Of the transformations Townsend (1990, 36) examines in his study of "Spoken Prague Czech," the *v*- prefix "varies the most among speakers and is the most dependent on the speaker's background, education, their mood at the moment, whom they are talking to, where they are, what they are talking about; in other words, the whole context of the utterance, including its relation to other words in the sentence."

Over the course of years of hearing this term, I came to realize that *vono*, in the context of Czech bluegrass musicking, is what people want to experience, or what it is that they are aiming for, striving toward. *Vono* is thus, understandably, as slippery as a greased pig. It can be articulated as an affirmation. Luthier Ondřej "Ondra" Holoubek, in emphasizing the importance of doing one's utmost, stressed that musicians and luthiers should work "aby to bylo fakt jako vono" (so that it would really be *vono*).[13]

Vono is often (perhaps more often) heard as part of a negative identification or a critique, complaint, or grumble. There are a number of excellent Czech-language texts that have been drafted to fit with the melody of the (US) bluegrass standard "Carolina in the Pines," but according to banjoist Petr

Hejkal, when Czechs sing these translations instead of the original English, "už to není vono" (that's not *vono* anymore). Fiddler Rostislav Fischer, in describing his difficulties learning to bow in stylistically appropriate ways, said of his right-hand technique as a beginning fiddler, "nebylo to vono" (that wasn't *vono*). In describing younger musicians who play in the driving style of the Plzeň-based band Cop, venerable Czech banjoist Marko Čermák asserted that while "oni mysleji ze to je vono" (they think it is *vono*), he prefers older American bluegrass bands that produced a gentler, more relaxed sound.[14]

I call this *vono* the "it" that Czech bluegrassers are trying to perform, their way of articulating "the balance between music as a marker of style and music in practice" (Kisliuk and Gross 2004, 259). In pursuing bluegrass and its "ostensibly unchanging" genre, sound, and style, Czechs constantly forge their own idea of what *vono* is and isn't.

According to Townsend (1990, 37–38), Czechs "may use [the *v*- prefix] with full force only with expressive or emotionally colored words," or with words for domestic things, plants, or animals and other common, everyday terms. Merely calling something "it" in a specific, locally significant way can thus set it apart as new or worthy of note—or just the opposite: as the most proximate, familiar, and frequently used. Alexei Yurchak's (2006, 128) explanation of the concept of *vnye* (a Russian word meaning "inside/outside") in the context of the last decades of Soviet socialism reflects a similar sense of "being simultaneously inside and outside of some context—such as, being within a context while remaining oblivious of it, imagining yourself elsewhere, or being inside your own mind."

As an outsider, I have learned to negotiate the kinds of binary distinctions that my Czech bluegrasser colleagues face. Bluegrass can be foreign or domestic, sung in English or Czech; even if it is not called "Czech bluegrass," it still includes some aspects of those two terms and the web of meaning they bring together. Some aspects of what Czech bluegrassers do can be appreciated because of their Czechness, such as centuries-old traditions of instrument making. Other aspects of Czechness might be less welcome, such as a vocal accent while singing an English lyric—for example, the consonant pair *th* is frustratingly difficult for Czechs to pronounce. In terms of translation, all of these phenomena could be seen as "deformations"—mistakes in the process of making bluegrass Czech.

On a more positive note, much of what is perceived as "American" in bluegrass is very welcome for Czech bluegrassers—with some caveats. Czechs may acknowledge the value of a particular form or aspect of bluegrass but not give it priority in what they do as bluegrassers. For instance, a musician may focus on contemporary progressive banjo styles, but likely will still value early stylists such as Earl Scruggs and Don Reno. In a more pointed example, a bluegrasser might not value the racist legacy of blackface minstrelsy, but acknowledges it as part of the cultural history of US string band music.

These contrasts present differentiable elements: foreign/domestic, difficult to master/easy to do. The boundaries are not always so easy to draw in what I call Americanism, the practice of re-creating aspects of US culture outside the United States. Americanisms as I have observed them in the Czech Republic are not confined to music, and are seldom easy to categorize in terms of nationality. For instance, is an American Willys jeep that was left in the Czech city of Plzeň during the 1945 withdrawal of Patton's army and has

An American military jeep owned and restored (and certified for driving on Czech roads) by banjoist Luděk "Wolfi" Brancuzsky, Luka nad Jihlavou, Czech Republic, 2009.

been painstakingly restored and maintained by a Czech militaria enthusiast over the decades—using a combination of scrounged American, Czech, and Russian parts—a Czech object or an American one?

Czech musical Americanisms have a similarly tangled provenance. Thus, as I approached my research fieldwork, my perceived status as a "native speaker" of bluegrass meant that I couldn't find a straightforward way to follow Mantle Hood's (1960) paradigm of researching by becoming "bimusical" through study with a "native" master musician. Many of the Czech musicians I met, especially early on in my fieldwork, were intimidated by my "native" American/bluegrasser status—and wanted to take lessons from *me*. Ironically, I couldn't serve as an "insider" instructor for many Czechs, as I have a limited set of bluegrass competencies myself.

In the end, I have focused my research on the issues that arise in carrying out bluegrass-related activities within a Czech context, regardless of ability or professional status. While I have spent time with skilled Czech musicians, I have undertaken informal apprenticeships with people who may not be master musicians but are virtuosic at having fun with bluegrass, with procuring information and materials to further their musical/community projects, with renovating the world they live in through bluegrass activity. I have gained a sense of what it is like to be part of today's flourishing (if complicated and often cantankerous) Czech bluegrass community. In the pages that follow, I first provide a background for Czech Americanism and indicate some of the roots of Czech bluegrass music. The following chapters present case studies in which I show how Czech bluegrassers find obstacles and opportunities in their negotiation of Czechness and Americanness: in marketing their performances and products, in playing the fiddle, and in singing gospel songs.

My attention to ways of "being Czech bluegrass" emerges from my understanding of music as a process rather than an artifact, as a relationship rather than a thing. The most profound and significant moments of my music making as a researcher have been in intimate situations like interviews, band rehearsals, and jam sessions, in which musical sounds are woven into a larger fabric of sociality and discourse. As my colleagues invited me into these moments, my apprenticeship extended (as apprenticeships tend to) outside the realm of simple instruction, blurring the boundaries between Czech and American, between work and play, self and other—doing just what music always does.

2

CZECH BLUEGRASS HISTORIES AND BACKGROUNDS

APPROACHING CZECHNESS

Czech bluegrass, while part of a globalized discourse on bluegrass music, is nevertheless uniquely *Czech*. Making this statement has sometimes gotten me in trouble with Czech bluegrassers, as the following anecdote shows.

> Petr Brandejs, banjoist, bandleader, pedagogue, long-time president of the Czech bluegrass association, and an all-around nice guy, was perturbed when I told some other folks at our lunch table that I was researching, as I put it, "*český* bluegrass."[1] With this term I was referring to what was going on around us at the bluegrass workshop that Petr helped organize and teach. "But this is *American* bluegrass," he protested. I posed my typical response to this insistence that the music itself is American: the *activity* that creates these sounds is Czech. We were sitting in the middle of a hundred Czech people who were all learning from other Czechs how to perform this music. So much of the weekend workshop in the little town of Malé Svatoňovice was Czech: from the *kulturní dům* (house of culture) on the square that hosted the big jam on Saturday night to the food we had all just loaded onto trays at the *jídelna* (cafeteria) of the local *střední odborné učiliště* (a sort of applied high school where folks train for jobs such as waiters, hoteliers, mechanics, and bodyguards). As part of Brandejs's Fall Bluegrass Workshop, we were all singing, playing, and listening to bluegrass, with many hands wrapped around

headstocks labeled Gibson and Martin as well as Čapek, Lebeda, and Průcha.[2] At this point, the conversation stalled. Neither of us—nor the other teachers sitting at the table—could resolve the problem. And neither Brandejs nor I was willing to concede. I took the standstill as a truce—maybe we are both right: all this activity is somehow both American *and* Czech.[3]

Petr Brandejs's protestations notwithstanding, Czech bluegrass music making and other Czech practices of Americanism are parts of a generations-deep process that has spread to all corners of the Czech lands. These phenomena are naturalized as "Czech" and are not experienced as "foreign." More specifically, they are not essentially or primarily foreign. They feel like "home" to Czechs, yet these activities and sounds are versions of a distinctly Czech Americanness—or Czech Americanism.

Czech bluegrass is the result of Czechs pursuing their musical projects in the midst of a three-way dialectic between ideas about national and ethnic identity, musical and discursive practices, and immediate and media-enabled relationships and communities. These categories often blur and connect, in no small part because music making is a series of actions, the work of people in relationship. Here I extend this idea by presenting Czech bluegrass as a process that also proceeds through the actions of people in history, circling around the question of not just *what* Czech bluegrass is and where it came from, but *how* Czechs have made bluegrass Czech, and in turn become part of bluegrass themselves.

TRAMPING AND EARLY AMERICANISM

Many Czech bluegrassers ground their histories in the history of tramping, a practice that began in the early twentieth century and mixes outdoor recreation with elements borrowed from the American West. Tramping is a key part of Czech life and history, and *trampské písničky* (tramp songs) are the foundation of Czech bluegrass and country music making. At the beginning of his account of Czech folk and country music—appropriately titled *Legendy folku a country* (Legends of folk and country)—television producer and pop-culture historian Jiří Vondrák (Vondrák and Skotal 2004, 11) quotes a joke by banjoist Jarda Čvančara that connects his subject to a grander historical legend: "[T]he first Czech who claimed a right to country was Bedřich Smetana: after all, he wrote 'My Country' and put an Indian in his opera *The Bartered Bride*. This is further proof that all this had already started in 1860."[4] Vondrák's quip is not that far off the mark; "America" served as a conceptual play space for European imaginations long before bluegrass.[5] Antonín

Dvořák might lay a more substantial claim to first intertwining "Czech" and "American" musicalities because of his composition and pedagogical work in the United States (Beckerman 2003).

Another nineteenth-century Czech who contributed to a more informed Czech conception of the United States was Vojtěch Náprstek, a journalist and social reformer whose accounts of frontier adventures and the life of Czechs in the United States informed, entertained, and connected Czechs in the homeland and in the United States alike (Šolle 1990). Tomáš Garrigue Masaryk, an acquaintance of Náprstek, would have visited the Prague salon and the Náprstek Museum, where Náprstek's artifacts and papers are still housed. Masaryk played a role in Czech connections to the United States both personally and governmentally. He adopted his middle name as part of his marriage to American heiress Charlotte Garrigue; as first president of the Czechoslovak Republic in 1918, he sought favorable relations with the Wilson administration as Europe reorganized after World War I.

German author Karl May provided another source of information about and images of the United States, one that was less grounded in reality than those of Náprstek and Masaryk, but has likely been more popular. May's novels about the "Wild West" were first published around 1900 and soon spread stories of exploits by ace frontiersman "Old Shatterhand" and the Apache sage "Winnetou" throughout central Europe.[6] Despite his extensive popularity throughout much of Europe, May is relatively unknown in the United States—possibly due to his rooting in German and European culture, his anti-Americanism and possible antisemitism, and his sheer "irrelevance" (Sammons 1998, 246–256).[7]

Music was a key part of budding Czech Americanism. Vondrák (Vondrák and Skotal 2004, 11) posits that the "first contact with American folk song" happened when Czech legionnaires serving with Russia during World War I encountered US soldiers. Military encounters would continue as a means for cultural contact. Joseph "Buřt" Braun, an aging "tramp," also cites the classic "modern" trauma of that war as part of the impetus for the Czech tramping phenomenon: "When our boys returned from the First World War, they were disturbed, they were young, they were eighteen, nineteen, twenty years old, and they were looking for something different. That's why they went out into nature, and their example was Jack London.[8] And that's why these tramp camps emerged. And the names of these camps were taken from these books, from films" (Vondrák and Skotal 2004, 12). As Braun indicates, actual landscapes have been significant for Czech recreation practices. Anthropologist Melinda Reidinger (2007, 23) traces the roots of the Czech tradition of weekend cottaging (and associated practices such as hiking, gardening, and boating) to the establishment of Bohemia as the industrial heart of the Austro-Hungarian Empire in the eighteenth century. As cities, factories, and extractive industries expanded, so did the means to escape them and their impact on the land, and to appreciate what Reidinger calls "the restorative power of nature, of landscape and of tradition" (29).

Through the early twentieth century, the global desire for respite from the developing city led to quasi-military and nationalist expressions such as the Scouting movement and the German *Wandervögel*, which paralleled family-oriented tourism sites in the United States such as the national parks and the YMCA's "Indian Guides" program.[9] While there were many Czech scouts (or *skauti*), and Sokol athletic/community groups had been active through the nineteenth century, Czechs also sought less organized recreations and the freedom and individual expression that tramping afforded.[10]

Folklore, philosophy, and fiction are cited as formative influences on tramping: Jack London's 1907 memoir *The Road* is often cited as the source of the term itself.[11] Tramp fun was further colored by stories of the Wild West from novelists such as London and Zane Grey, as well as films that featured early film cowboys like Tom Mix. Tramps also used elements of Native American culture. Settlements (*osady*) with names like "Jukon," "Colorado," and "Kansas" featured cabins and wigwams constructed with instructions taken from the Native American–oriented woodcraft books of Ernest Thompson Seton. Miloš Seifert acknowledged the influence of Seton's *Book of Woodcraft* on the title page of his 1920 book *Through Nature and Life towards Pure Humanity*.[12] Seifert followed Seton in turning away from the military structure of Scouting, calling for a woodcraft practice that drew instead from knowledge of Native American life and lore.

In her study of tramping during the interwar period (1918–1938), Reidinger (2007) critiques histories of Czech Americanism and nature-oriented recreations that pose these endeavors as proletarian; she finds that tramps were often from middle-class backgrounds, if not educated and moneyed elites—dressing and acting as if they were working class.[13] Americanism was part of the play of inversion, with cowboy, sailor, and gold prospector common costume choices.

The ideals of tramping, in any case, were often lofty. Tramp historian Pavel Jirásek, after citing Rousseau's influence on early tramps, also named two "spiritual friends" who influenced tramping through their intellectual thought and action, "the American transcendentalist Ralph Waldo Emerson and his student, also a great idealist, that pragmatic artist of life Henry David Thoreau. Where the first—philosopher, aestheticist, and a great essayist—came with a mystical vision of perfect beauty and moral nature, the second actually left the city and lived altogether freely for several years in the woods at Walden" (Jirásek 1999). The venerable chronicler of Czech tramping Josef Peterka, who wrote under the pseudonym "Bob Hurikán," cites Thoreau, Emerson, and other philosophers as crucial to tramp philosophy in his *History of Tramping* (Hurikán 1990). Thus tramps—Braun's former soldiers and Reidinger's bourgeois dandies alike—were participating in a global response to industrialization, urbanization, and popular culture that included philosophy and scholarship, popular adventure writing, and films—as well as music.

The term *trampská píseň* (tramp song) refers to a musical practice that shows strong US influence and creative Czech imagination. In a history and analysis of tramp song, musicologist Josef Kotek (1995) describes the flow of American popular culture into the Czech imagination as a "flood," one that inspired first imitation, and then innovation. By 1922, Kotek reports, composer and author Jaroslav Mottl had produced the tramp song "Cariboo," and tramping had a full-fledged musical accompaniment (168). Kotek gives as an example of the sounds that inspired Czechs the 1925 recording "Dinah" by the Revelers, who according to Gage Averill (2003, 81) were one of the last white groups performing the barbershop style that flourished in the early 1900s. This reference, as well as the primacy of male ensemble vocal performance in tramp music making, indicates that American groups were a strong influence on Czech tramping-related close-harmony singing (Kotek 1995, 173).

The Supraphon recording company's compilation *Trampské písně 1920–1939* (2002) is where I first heard the sounds that further reveal the globalized nature of popular music of the period. The recording of "Ukolébavka námořníka" (Sailor's lullaby) by the group Settlers Club features O. Kovář playing the *havajská kytara* (Hawaiian guitar) as an introduction to the minor-mode 3/4-time piece. The Czech lands are landlocked, so this "island" sound would accord with the Czech romantic affinity for nautical images and themes. The musically exotic elements in tramp music were part of a larger worldwide vogue: the ukulele, the slide or "steel" guitar, and other Hawaiian artifacts and practices gained prominence in other locales during the first decades of the 1900s (Troutman 2013, 29–31). The early country music star Jimmie Rodgers, for instance, gained some fame early on with groups that featured a "Hawaiian steel guitar" and songs like "Everybody Does It in Hawaii" (Felske and Rasporich 2004, 193).

In their heyday during the interwar period, tramp songs were central to the mainstream of popular music. Another genre that shared this position in the Czech media world was a folk-inflected song form called *lidovka*. Where *lidovka* blended art song with Czech folkloric images and traditionalist melodies, tramp music touted its connections to the West. In his analysis of the "genre and structural characteristics" of tramp songs, Kotek (1995, 176) distinguishes this repertory from the contemporary *lidovka*, especially its "jazz" influence and the use of the prevailing "new, modern dance rhythms" such as the classic foxtrot, tango, and waltz.

IMAGINED FOLKLORES

The flourishing of tramping and tramp song within Czech society underscores the problem of "folklore" in Bohemia, especially in the region surrounding Prague. I have heard Czechs cite a lack of local folklore as one reason for the vitality of Czech bluegrass. The patchwork of microregions in Moravia, each with its own *kroj* (folk costume), dialects, and dance and song styles, presents a different situation. Antonín Dvořák and other collectors/arrangers of folkloric music drew heavily on these regions, more than they did from the western part of the Czech-speaking lands.

In the heartland of Bohemia, around Prague, there are fewer distinctively folkloric practices to celebrate. The South Bohemian Strakonice bagpipe traditions and the songs of the Chodsko region located near Domažlice on the western border with Germany are exceptions to this dearth of notable musical folklore (Markl 1963). A wider frame would include urban folkloric practices such as *staropražské lidové písničky* (old Prague people's songs), of which many were composed by Karel Hašler, which are comparable to the nineteenth-century music forms *Wienerlied* and *Schrammelmusik*, preserved in Vienna. Even within these genres, bluegrass is at play: Petr Kůs, a prominent member of Prague's bluegrass community, has played bass for Šlapeto, one of the main groups playing old Prague songs.[14]

The nature of "folklore" is worth noting, as "folkness" here intersects with other negotiations of otherness. Remember that Jiří Vondrák cited Czech exposure to "American folk song" as the inspiration for Czech tramping, and thus for the folk and country music that was to follow. In appropriating cultural elements from the distant United States (as well as the mainstream of current popular culture), Czech Americanists of the early twentieth century were being *modern* as they drew on a real or imagined past, as they took part in cosmopolitan discourses on "nature," and as they recovered from the traumas of modern life.[15] This situation gives a transnational spin to the paradigm described by Regina Bendix (1997, 8) in her critique of "authenticity" as a part of folklore and folklore studies, and "a peculiar longing, at once modern and antimodern. It is oriented toward the recovery of an essence whose loss has been realized only through modernity, and whose recovery is feasible only through methods and sentiments created in modernity."

Czechs involved in "Americanism" with a folklore focus (such as those involved with projects like the Náprstek Museum) can also be fruitfully considered part of the modern/antimodern tension, which historian T. J. Jackson Lears (1994, 301, 306, 305) has examined in Náprstek's US contemporaries who sought the "real" in art, writing, and thought. Lears adds to Bendix's critique of the "quest for authenticity" by arguing that "antimodern activists" invoked tradition, but often lapsed into "vitalist" pursuit of authentic experience as an end in itself, not a path to ultimate concerns and social welfare. Lears suspects that many American authenticity-seeking projects conceal "a desperate flight from a meaningless existence," especially when they focus on individual self-fulfillment.

Germanist scholar Jeffrey L. Sammons (1998, 231–235) examines this kind of self-interested representation in European reception of Karl May's adventure stories. Sammons finds that May often used a first-person narrator as a thinly disguised projection of the author himself, a projection that was often misleading. One of May's most well-known pseudobiographical narrator figures, from the novel *Winnetou*, eventually becomes known as "Old Shatterhand" for his ability to defeat opponents in hand-to-hand combat. Although he is described in an early chapter title as a "greenhorn," he has done enough book research at home in Germany before heading to the American West that he proves himself able to "outshoot, outride, outsurvey, and outthink the most experienced trapper or scout, outstalk and outwit the most skillful Indian" (231). Through this act of narrative salesmanship and "recursive, literal duplicity" (232), Sammons finds May thus selling, along with his stories, the authenticity of the real-life author of the stories.

This sort of duplicity, while unfortunate, does not eliminate the possibility of fruitful play. May's tendencies toward fictionalization *outside* of his writing (for instance, in insisting that he had traveled to the US during a period when records show that he was in prison for fraud) do not make his published stories any less effective as inspiration. Late in May's life, many highlights of his self-constructed autobiography were challenged and for the most part shown to be fictitious. Still, Winnetou and Shatterhand stories have continued to sell, and have inspired numerous live performances, film and television productions, and even theme parks (Sammons 1998; Frayling 2006, 103–120; Weber 2012).

This culture of imagination worked in dialectic with the sort of "ethnography" that Náprstek supported, and which was used to inform Indianism. In an essay on the 1895 Czechoslavic Ethnographic Exhibition, anthropologist Andrew Lass (1989) traces modern ideologies and conceptions of Czechness and of "Czech folk culture" (7) in questioning Czech imaginative ideas about culture and identity. Evoking present-day concerns of identity politics, Lass argues that Czech notions of an "other" circa 1900 were supported by constructions of *českost* (Czechness) based on exclusion of non-Czech groups such as Germans and Roma (gypsies) and on Czechs' desire for autonomy within the Austro-Hungarian Empire, to which they were subject until 1918 (15). Czechs indeed drew selectively from outside culture in establishing their own way of being at home through tramping and other Americanism-related projects. The role of media (including books, radio, music, and films) in providing fuel for these imaginative projects would only grow as the twentieth century continued. The ways in which politics, aesthetics, and practicalities shaped media flows through the mid-1900s would define how bluegrass became a central part of Czech Americanism.

MEDIA AND APPROPRIATION

The Second World War marks a watershed moment for Czech popular music, especially in the sources through which Czechs accessed American pop culture. Records, radio, and other media came to even greater prominence as Czechs' ability to travel was limited by the Communist Party–controlled government. The brief period between the end of the war in 1945 and the accession of the Communist Party to power in 1948 saw a return to the jazz and jazz-inflected popular music of the interwar era, and some of the access to media that enabled Czech Americanism. The ability of Czechs to learn about US media and their ability to play a part in global mediascapes would evolve in the following decades, as the history of bluegrass shows.

Josef Škvorecký (1979) offers perspectives on the postwar transitional period as well as the surrounding periods of Nazi and communist suppression of jazz. Pop music scholar Aleš Opekar (1998) points to the most important means by which Czechs accessed popular music in the decades that followed the war: foreign radio stations. I will quote Opekar at length as he tells a story that is strikingly similar to narratives I have heard from Czech bluegrassers:

> The most important medium for spreading American popular music in the 50s to our country were foreign radio stations. The first was AFN Munich, American Forces Network, broadcasting to American soldiers based in Germany, thus broadcasting to the young, both black and white. Later Radio Luxembourg was more popular and widespread.
>
> Most of [the] Czech and Slovak rock musicians were influenced by those radio stations. A lot of fans wrote lists of music they heard or tried to understand and write the lyrics. Several enthusiasts illegally produced homemade gramophone records. They bought old equipment from the original small private gramophone producers who were active before 1948. The pirate producers

> used originally discarded X-rays, later also other materials. They made records from the mentioned western radio stations or they made also pirate copies of foreign records which rarely occurred in the country. . . .
>
> First tape recorders on Czech market in the end of the 50[s] were very expensive for normal people and the list of owners of the tape recorders was registered at the police stations and the police was allowed to confiscate the tapes with "inappropriate" records. In spite of this danger a lot of private parties were held in Prague with country music, rockabilly, and later rock'n'roll music from tapes and from homemade gramophone records. These homemade gramophone records were sold on the black market and were eagerly purchased especially by merry-go-round and fair operators. In this way the rock'n'roll recordings even found their way to small towns and villages where it was not available to tune into a Western radio station. (1998, 351)

Opekar links this influx of media with the continued development of Americanist musical activity. He explains that tramp singing in particular was key to the adoption of newer musical forms: "Almost all Czech [rock and pop] guitarists grew up from [the] tramping movement playing tramping songs on a Spanish guitar at the campfire" (354).

The emergence of industries to provide the equipment needed for the growing Czech folk, country, and rock scenes in the postwar period was not interrupted by the Communist Party's assumption of power. Opekar gives a brief history of the Dřevokov firm in the town of Blatná in South Bohemia, indicating that Czech instrument builders quickly adapted to the new technology of postwar popular music in spite of Cold War limitations on travel and communication. The Dřevokov firm not only provided instruments at home, but marketed them abroad:

> First product from 1950 was the Hawaii[an] guitar with the name "Accord." The first electric guitar was produced in 1954 under the name "Grazioso." The huge success at the world exhibition Expo 1958 in Brussels, with a gold medal, opened the world market. . . . Roughly four years of exporting the guitars under the name "Futurama Foreign" to the west including England caused that the electric guitar from Blatná was in the hands of such people as Buddy Holly, George Harrison, or Jimmy Page. (Opekar 1998, 352)

The exporting of guitars was a government-approved effort that showcased Czechoslovak preeminence in musical instrument manufacture. The importing of Western sounds was more common, however.

As rock and roll captured the ears of Czech listeners and musicians, country music (including bluegrass) made similar inroads. In describing the radio schedule of the American Forces Network in Munich, radio researcher R. Stephen Craig (1988, 310) lists "*Hillbilly Gasthaus*, a program of what was at that time described as mountain music." Craig reports that this program "drew thousands of letters from German listeners who praised it as a prime example of American folk music," a response that would likely have been echoed by Czech listeners if they had been able to write from behind the iron curtain. Marko Čermák recalls hearing a country music show during the 1950s, broadcast from US military radio in Munich—likely the long-running *Stickbuddy Jamboree*, which in the early 1960s featured deejay Wagon Wheel Willie.[16]

US government–sponsored broadcasts were popular in the Czech Republic, so much so that the authorities worked to jam and otherwise disrupt incoming radio programs, especially those containing pointedly political content broadcast in the Czech language. Journalist Richard Cummings (2009) provides an account of the Eastern Bloc's efforts to combat the aggressive propaganda broadcasts of Radio Free Europe/Radio Liberty, including tales of intrigue (and even assassination!), which seem a world away from the music cases I examine, but took place in some of the same bandwidth.

In his investigation of foreign radio reception in the USSR, anthropologist Alexei Yurchak (2006) finds that authorities there would jam Russian-language broadcasts from the Voice of America and Radio Liberty, as they were overtly critical of Soviet policies. Broadcasts in the original foreign languages (including, Yurchak states, the Voice of America in its English-language broadcast) were seldom jammed, and were part of the regular listening habits even of Russians faithful to the regime. "Listening regularly to all sorts of foreign stations"—not just the official Russian ones—"was not necessarily perceived as in contradiction to being a good Soviet person" because being "modern" and cosmopolitan was perceived as a good thing (181). The Czech connoisseurship of folk and country forms, including bluegrass, could in this light be seen both as countercultural and as accepted by the official culture. There would continue to be many such seeming contradictions in Czech transformations of country and bluegrass.

IMITATION AND THE BANJO

According to Opekar (1988, 354), "the pioneer period of Czech rock'n'roll is based on slavish copying and imitation. The copying of [a] foreign model was not considered as a shame, but a deliberate credo. In a preserved interview from 1963 with Evžen Fiala, leader of a band [called] Hell's Devils, the musician answered the question about their inspiration: 'We take songs over

[from] western singers because we are trying to be original.'" At first glance, Fiala's statement about being original through imitation seems paradoxical. The desire to be original and the possibility of imitating American music both had value for Czechs exploring bluegrass sounds during communism. The accounts of early Czech banjoist Marko Čermák and the succession of Czech bluegrassers who followed him show that imitation—specifically imitation of commercial audio recordings—has been a principal means of learning bluegrass, and participation remains part of a new and unique music scene.

The mixing of imitation, media, and learning is probably not surprising to many bluegrassers (both in the United States and elsewhere); Robert Cantwell's (1993, 6) discussion of mimesis as rooted in "impersonation" sheds light on the sorts of processes that contextualize Fiala's mixture of mimicry and originality. Cantwell indicates that "impersonation" can be a means of *self*-realization, echoing a theme that Melinda Reidinger (2007, 13–14) has identified in Czech Americanist re-creations.

Americanism has become a significant part not only of personal experience, but of the "collective imaginative remembering" intrinsic to Czechness (Connerton 1989, 21). The following stories told by Marko Čermák about his early interactions with bluegrass-related music (as well as those told about him by others) are further examples of the ways in which Czech mimetic projects resulted in multifaceted and imaginative "rememberings" of American music and the process by which it became "Czech." As he explained, "I am attempting to fully tell from my perspective the basic facts about the time, which presignified today's popularity of the five-string banjo here,[17] and approximate the inimitable atmosphere in which it all played out" (Čermák 1998, 17).

Čermák is a key figure in the establishment of bluegrass-related music making in the Czech Republic. His iconicity for Czech banjo music is tied to Pete Seeger's 1964 tour of the Czech Republic. During Seeger's tour, Čermák was fulfilling his mandatory military service and heard the sound of Seeger's banjo on a Czech radio broadcast. One of Seeger's concerts in Prague has been released on compact disc under the title *Pete Seeger in Prague, 1964* (Seeger 2001).[18]

Čermák's story has become a legendary narrative in the Czech bluegrass community. His recollections as they appear in his combination memoir/banjo instruction manual/songbook *Banjo z mlžných lesů* (Banjo from the foggy woods) (Čermák 1998) provide important background and fill in many details missing from the typical version of the story of his hearing Seeger's performance on the radio and then building a banjo according to photos taken at the 1964 concert. For one thing, Čermák places the important turning point in his life much earlier than 1964, in July 1956, when he was sitting by a friend's radio set and first heard the sounds that would change his life:

> From Pavel's radio resounded that strange English, and then in the next moment the banjo—fantastic, devilish, interpolated with the whinnying of horses. I probably stopped breathing, and my heart must have stopped. Then there were songs about cowboys; they played mandolins, violin, harmonica, guitars—all instruments that I knew well from cabins, from pubs, from the campfire. Now *that* was really music, it really grooved [*šlapalo*]. And that fantastic banjo. I knocked over my chair and begged Pavel to turn it up, but unfortunately, "Someone would blow the whistle on us," he said. "These are programs for American soldiers who serve in Germany—Radio Munich." That was it, it was decided. From that day on, wherever we were, we found our way to his radio. (9)

Čermák relates his subsequent infatuation with the banjo: the process by which he eventually bought a four-string "tenor" banjo at a used instrument store in Prague. On later tramping adventures he met fellow American music fans, including Honza Vyčítal, who would join him in the seminal group the Greenhorns.

For these tramps, music helped translate the sorts of fun they enjoyed during weekends spent around a campfire in the woods into a form they could enjoy back in their urban weekday environment. Čermák eventually found a group that met at a pub in the Prague district of Smíchov on Wednesdays, a serial moment of tramp bliss that he called "[a] wondrous little Czech America in the middle of the building up of socialism" (1998, 12). At these gatherings, Čermák continued his search for information about the banjo, meeting Czech tenor banjoist and songster Kapitán Kid and playing in the top Dixieland circles in Prague. He learned jazz techniques in which a plectrum or flat pick is used to strum all or most of the strings while the left hand stops the strings to produce a series of quick-moving chord changes. These techniques, however, did not produce the sounds Čermák was looking for: banjo strings plucked in repeated patterns that shifted in kaleidoscopic syncopation. He was searching for something completely unlike what Czechs were playing, for the sort of playing he heard on US military radio, and which he linked to the American West: "I felt that these songs simply had to have a banjo. But some other way, not like in Dixieland. So I tried desperately to play like those Americans who played for the American soldiers. I doubled my plectrum, nothing. I doubled the strings on the tenor banjo—nothing . . . still just dixieland, not cowboy banjo" (12).

In an interview, Čermák explained that he placed a small block of wood between two normal flat picks to double the notes he could hit with a single playing stroke of his right hand—a harebrained idea that reveals, in his words, how "desperate" he was to find out how to get that special banjo sound.[19] Note Čermák's early-1960s mixing of the cowboy image with the sounds of southeastern US string band music. This elision is a result of the midcentury marketing of "hillbilly" music as part of the interest in the Wild West and cowboys that scholars such as Richard Peterson (1997) have outlined, another example of the imaginative creativity that has framed Czech re-creations of bluegrass.

Čermák did eventually see Pete Seeger's instrument in photos taken at the 1964 Prague concert and had his illuminating moment: the instrument had five strings! He quickly constructed his own banjo (with contributions from his army comrades' carpentry and metalworking skills), but he was still a long way from emulating the sounds he so desired. He soon was playing his unique instrument with the Greenhorns, and then with the group White Stars. He knew there was a lot more to learn; it was another experience that brought the final important pieces of technique together. One day in 1967, as Čermák tells the story,

> Jarda Čvančara called to say that at the Fučíkárna there was an American fashion show, and someone there was playing the five-string banjo.[20] I flew to get a ticket and a translator, Jarda Čvančara's brother. Indeed, at the presentation of Strauss jeans, a musician who had until that point been playing electric guitar picked up a five-string banjo, which until then had been lying behind him on the ground. . . . He played real bluegrass, exactly what I had heard on that German radio station fifteen years earlier. I couldn't wait until the women had stopped presenting and I shakily knocked on the door of the dressing room. (1998, 18)

The banjoist was Bob Yellin, who had played with the Greenbriar Boys, an early urban bluegrass band from the New York City area that in the 1960s also featured Eric Weissberg (known for recording the banjo for the 1971 film *Deliverance*) and Ralph Rinzler (a folklorist also known for his work representing bluegrass bandleader Bill Monroe, and as an arts administrator and advocate in Washington, DC). Marko, ignorant of all this context, was simply thrilled to meet an American banjoist in person.

> It was a shock. He brought out a real American banjo, put it in my hands, and showed me his finger picks. But only three, he didn't use the ring finger.[21] He laughed, astonished, when he saw my [picks], jerry-rigged and soldered together from a lunchmeat can. . . . Bob gave me his, and also some strings. He was fascinated when he saw the accessories I was using to play. And he played—fabulously American. . . . He sent me [Earl] Scruggs's [banjo]

> instruction book . . . he sent three LPs, from which I retexted a whole bunch of pieces for the White Stars. (19)

While Čermák is a revered figure because of the work he has done to understand and present banjo music as a performer, contemporary Czechs also add counterstories. According to one such story, for example, Jiří Tichota of the band Spirituál Kvintet was the first real five-string banjo owner in the Czech Republic—which is interesting, in that Tíchota is not a bluegrass-type player. Čermák himself has drifted away from the bluegrass community that has drawn so much inspiration from him. His more recent music making, which he often describes as "old-time," fits more within the tramp song tradition. In the imagination of Czech bluegrass history, however, Čermák's position in stories remains similar to that of Bill Monroe, the self-proclaimed "father of bluegrass music": people consider Čermák to have played a central role in making bluegrass Czech.

Czech American studies scholar Eva Škrobáková (2002) has compiled an outline of the history of bluegrass, in which she describes some of the Czech history of the music, highlighting the eclectic approach to it taken by musicians from Čermák's generation. In her writing, she refers to the early-era activity as bluegrass-related; recordings of such groups as the Rangers/Plavcí, the Bluegrass Hoppers/Fešácí, Bobři/Beavers, and Kamarádí taborových ohně/Friends of the Campfire indicate the wide variety of interpretations of bluegrass in the 1960s and 1970s.[22] Škrobáková's account emphasizes the importance of the sounds of individual instruments, the technique used to play them, and the instrumental lineup as a whole to the creation of a bluegrass sound and a "bluegrass performance":

> I [have] labeled these bands "bluegrass-related," because on the one hand they used [the] bluegrass line-up (banjo, mandolin, guitar, fiddle and double bass; dobro was virtually unknown then), but their sound was quite different from American bluegrass. It was because they did not know how to approach the instruments in order to achieve the "right" sound, but moreover, it was usually nearly impossible to get the sound from their instruments. In other words, it was not only the five-string banjo that was obscure then. The guitars and the mandolins used by our pickers were also quite different from the American ones. The mandolin played by Bill Monroe was modified and produced by the *Gibson* company in the early 1920s and it differed from the usual Italian model in a number of elements: it had [an] arched top and back (but the back was not so bulging as the old Italian type), instead of the oval hole it had a couple of violin-like F-holes, the bridge was adjustable, and the most important was the new shape, according to which we recognise pear-shaped

> "A" type and decorative "F" type, which is more expensive and preferred by bluegrass musicians. Therefore similarly to the story about the banjo: how could our pickers [be] aware of [the] existence of such an instrument? And how could they achieve the typical "barking" and "chopping" bluegrass sound from their old classical mandolins? The guitar used then by the tramps was the mellow-sounding classical type, which was also taken over by the bluegrass players. And again the sound was quite different from the full vigorous tone and especially the full backup sound of the American big-body "dreadnought" type, usually made by the Martin Company. In the sixties, the tramps started to use the sharp sounding jazz guitar (called "džibsonka") which sometimes appeared in bluegrass bands, too. At least the violins and contrabasses were more [or] less the same. Nowadays, the sound of the 1960s' bands is usually referred to as "trampgrass." (2002, 38)

Škrobáková's account conveys a sense of Czechs' exuberance in this period as they slowly discovered the instruments and techniques that were necessary for the bluegrass sound and style. The label *džibsonka*, a transformation of "Gibson," is a good example of the kind of "transitional" labels that emerged from this process of discovery. The *dž* sound in Czech is often substituted for foreign sounds like the soft *g* and *j* (for example *bendžo* as a common phonetic transformation of "banjo"). Here the *dž* sound is used for a soft *g* sound, a Czech mispronunciation of the famous musical instrument company's name, which in the United States is pronounced with a hard *g*.

NORMALIZATION, COTTAGING, AND ACCOMMODATION

Despite the hiccups and misunderstandings that hindered pioneers like Marko Čermák, the first era of Czech bluegrass-related music bloomed through the 1960s in the thaw of the so-called "Prague Spring." The reforming efforts of First Secretary of the Communist Party Alexander Dubček and a loosening of state control and surveillance coincided with the influx of American popular music sounds, creating conditions for Czech bluegrass to take root and flourish. This period also saw the Czech New Wave in cinema as well as other artistic and social developments that had been impossible in the previous decade. For Czechs, this thaw ended on August 21, 1968, when Soviet-led forces of the Warsaw Pact alliance rolled into the country, beginning a military occupation that would last until 1989.

Michael Elavsky (2005) has investigated the Czech music business under the post-invasion Soviet pressure to "normalize" Czechoslovakia with the state of things in the Soviet Union and the larger communist sphere, finding that the period in which Dubček's reforms were rolled back created a culture of censorship in the media and in Czechoslovak culture more widely. "Music clubs and theaters were closed, stipulations were placed on the images, sounds, and repertoires musical artists could employ and specifications were put in place regarding the conditions for performance and performances themselves. . . . Some artists accommodated the changes, while others chose to leave the country while they could." National borders were closed in 1969, and "artists were subsequently forced to make a choice; pay lip service to the regime and follow its rules so as to keep their job, or face official censure and its consequences for their musical creativity." Elavsky also describes some of the consequences of stepping out of line during this period of counter-reform. The public use of English was limited or forbidden in sung texts and in the names of bands, as were certain dance moves or on-stage or on-screen gestures. "Besides losing the right to perform, one could be forced into other less desirable occupations such as street sweeping, coal stoking, or sanitation collection, a fate that many artists and intellectuals suffered in the wake of the Warsaw Pact invasion" (103).

Elavsky's focus on rock and pop music does not entirely fit with the experience of Czechs involved with bluegrass-related music making.[23] The pressures he describes in their most severe forms affected only the professional musicians who, as part of the mandatory employment of the socialist state, were registered as working in the official musicians' union. For a few top bluegrass-related groups, there were changes made. For instance, Marko Čermák's Greenhorns changed their name to the Czech version of the word, Zelenáči. There are stories of musicians, promoters, and other music makers who were pressured to emigrate, especially in the 1980s, but most bluegrassers (and tramps) continued their Americanist play in the rural margins, in the safety of the woods, in tramp *osada* camps, and in private gatherings at homes and pubs.

The atmosphere of the mid-1970s through the mid-1980s was that of a tense standoff. Czechs tolerated the Soviet invaders and the "normalization" of society, and the authorities allowed ideologically marginal behavior as long as it did not create political and social disruption or otherwise challenge official discourse. The Oscar-winning film *Kolya* (1996) illustrates the end of this period well, depicting the range of emotional and official tensions that Czechs experienced.

In spite of (and in part because of) this environment, bluegrass music thrived. Already officially approved since the time Marko Čermák (1998, 15) first performed "songs of oppressed American workers" with his military service colleagues at a presentation of "Army Artistic Creativity," bluegrass and country music served as a medium for expression that could be expressed as a defiance of the regime, but also read as support for its principles. Some Czech old-timers gloat that they fooled the authorities by adapting their presentation of bluegrass to communist discourse. "We told them it was the music of the poor people, of the working-class," said Ivo Drbohlav, a scientist, lyricist, bandleader, and guitar player (Buff 2005).

Tramping and bluegrass continued through normalization in concert with "cottaging," a practice of recreation, investment, and well-being common in many parts of Europe, but with specific resonances with Americanism and resistance in the Czech context. Vacation cottages are visible throughout the Czech landscape, and are a significant part of the country's life and culture. Along with rented garden plots, mountain chalets, vineyards, and wine cellars, cottages are nonprimary residences or recreational sites that have provided Czechs (and many of their European neighbors) with an alternative space in which to recover from the work week, to make some extra income through selling garden produce, to enjoy being outdoors, to reconnect with family, and to grow and produce foodstuffs and beverages unobtainable in stores.

Anthropologist Melinda Reidinger (2007, 13) examines cottaging as a means for what her informants called *seberealizace* (self-realization). This is not a phrase I have heard often from Czech bluegrassers, but the ways in which Reidinger and her informants use this concept parallel how bluegrass-related music making has created "alternate social networks" (34) not only for recreation, but for survival—indeed, the two were often linked. Both cottaging and bluegrass are recreational in multiple meanings of the word. They can be transformative, almost ritual activities for the re-creation of self and community. For Czechs these forms of "play" are serious business. As Reidinger explains, "cottages have functioned in the double sense of the Czech *realita*, which signifies both real estate *and* reality, actuality or truth-in-being itself" (13–14). The effects of a century of tramping and cottaging activities—and the bluegrass-related activities that accompany them—"have rippled far beyond the 'selves' of the cottagers, and have deeply impacted the nation's politics, economy, ecology, and the character of rural landscapes" (14).

The "recreational objects" involved in tramping and bluegrass-related music making are sometimes real estate, but more often are necessarily portable and easily transported to the next event: banjos, mandolins, and guitars, in addition to recordings, instruction books, and other items that are part of bluegrass music making. But as Reidinger argues, the most important parts of the practice, and its most significant effects, are perceptible beyond these objects and their physical sounds—they are a truth-in-being that participants construct in sound and space.

In exploring the distant and recent history as well as the continuing Czech activity based in cottaging, Reidinger (2007, 34) has proposed a theoretical model to describe this sort of recreative activity in socialist Czechoslovakia. She critiques three major conceptions of the motivation for cottaging—escape, resistance, and accommodation—and proposes a more nuanced mode of understanding that I connect with bluegrass-related music making.

Reidinger (2007) poses the first model of escape as a stance taken by Western outsiders, or by dissidents at the margin of official Czechoslovak life during normalization. This is the model, she explains, that is most known to "Western Anglophones"; it involves a "retreat from hostile forces in society into 'private' domestic spheres of home, family and close friends, artistic expression, or household-based, or unofficial economic activity" (39). Reidinger argues that many Czech insiders who voice this view are anticommunist dissidents who link this model to a putative Czech lack of political backbone, and the absence of civil society.

Reidinger (2007, 43–44) adds an addendum to this first theory of "escape," identifying what she calls "the 'folk' version of the theory of internal immigration": "that people had cottages [and, I would add, created imagined worlds through bluegrass] during the normalization era because they could not travel outside their borders, or that . . . such travel was severely limited. In Richard Handler's phrase, this is the 'native rationalization' that is repeated ad infinitum without . . . supporting evidence. It also contradicts one of the cottagers' other basic assumptions, that [Czechs'] need for recreation in nature is primary (or primordial?), and that cottages satisfy this need. If this were so, cottages could not *also* be just a cheap substitute for democratic freedoms." The desires that Reindiger finds in cottagers' search for *seberealizace* seem similar to those that guide the quest of bluegrassers for a shifting and difficult-to-define *vono*—if nothing else, in their sometimes contradictory natures.

Reidinger also cites documentary photographer Pavel Štecha's work *U nás: 1968–1990 / In Our Country* in raising questions about the cottaging phenomenon and the ambiguity of Americanism as defiance or collaboration with the regime. Štecha asks, "Were we [as Czechs] condemned to escape to colonies of cottages, or did we earn them through continued defiance? Perhaps with our amateur building enthusiasm we were reacting to the impossibility of self-realization at our jobs" (Štecha 2001, 5, quoted in Reidinger 2007, 47).

In addressing these questions, Reidinger (2007, 50) suggests that cottaging can be seen as part of "resistance . . . towards the idea and realization of 'progress' in industrial and technological development" inherent in scouting, tramping, and other early twentieth-century pursuits. She concludes, "If Communism was especially strongly resisted by cottagers, perhaps this is because it was seen as the most insistent and aggressive vanguard of industrial modernity."

In describing the theory of "accommodation and compensation," Reidinger (2007, 52) quotes Benjamin Kuras (1996, 23), who in his *Czechs and Balances* describes how the regime made Czech life "dull and idiotic, but compared with the rest of the communist world, remarkably comfortable. There was hardly a family which had not built itself a second home in the country to escape to every weekend—starting at midday on Friday and ending at midday on Monday."

Historian Paulina Bren contends that the "compensation" was a disguised effort to defuse popular dissent. Bren argues that the post-1968 government itself "collaborated" in the burgeoning cottage culture because of

> the obvious political advantages to be gained if the cities emptied out during the weekends, splintering urban inhabitants amongst different country locales. As the regime had learned from the experience of the Prague Spring, political discontent translated into political resistance not in the villages but in the cities; dissatisfaction was transformed into political action not by agricultural workers by the cities' intellectuals and intelligentsia. Thus, *chata* [cottage] culture could ostensibly provide for a depoliticized, government-mediated escape into pastoral Bohemia and Moravia for those who sought solace from the trauma of "normalization." (2002, 125–126)

Journalist Timothy Garton Ash is even more critical of the way Czechs cooperated in the normalization of the 1970s and 1980s:

> Forgetting is the key to the so-called normalization of Czechoslovakia. In effect, the regime has said to the people: Forget 1968. Forget your democratic traditions. Forget that you were once citizens with rights and duties. Forget politics. In return we will give you a comfortable, safe life. There'll be plenty of food in the shops and cheap beer in the pubs. You may afford a car and even a little country cottage—and you won't have to work competitively. We don't ask you to believe in us or our fatuous ideology. By all means listen to the Voice of America and watch Austrian television (sotto voce: So do we). (1990, 62)

Czechs already had many of the consumer products that other socialist countries considered luxuries—mainly because of the wealth of the country when it entered socialism. After 1968, there was little more to buy or procure in terms of consumer goods, so people poured their resources, time, and effort into second homes and cottages, and into recreations or hobbies like bluegrass music making. In this light, the consumer items that Ash lists are less important than the ways in which Czechs *used* them. The practice of cottaging, Reidinger (2007, 59) argues, is in some ways the opposite of consumerism: unlike consumer products, which quickly lose value, cottage objects and hobbies grow in value over time, providing dividends in body, mind, and relationships, and even in real estate or the growing value of a high-quality musical instrument.

Reidinger (2007, 60) states that dissident-leaning descriptions (e.g., Ash 1990; Bren 2002) attribute "passivity, cowardice, or an unvirtuously narrow concern with one's own living standard" to Czechs, and that they do not account for Czechs' "accomplishments in transforming themselves, their social circles, and the land around them." In proposing her own model for understanding cottaging and other Czech recreative activities, Reidinger puts more energy into asking "how" and less into asking "why," the motivating question for the three models she critiques. Borrowing from Aleksandr Solzhenitsyn's *Gulag Archipelago* and John Donne's notion that "no man is an island," Reidinger poses cottaging as part of an alternate network, or archipelago, "a complex parallel and overlapping world with alternative systems of labor, exchange, and socialization . . . [that] provided conduits for goods, services, and even moral values to circulate when the 'official' channels would not or could not oblige" (62).

Bluegrassers, like cottagers, carried out their pursuits thanks to their archipelagoes, their networks of friends, family, and acquaintances. They obtained instruments from colleagues: a bassist in Jihlava told me that he had paid a pittance for two lovely double basses that a friend had found while clearing out the local school's storage closets. And Marko Čermák described to me how his boss turned a blind eye to the banjo he kept—and practiced on—at work.

These examples indicate that the systems of alternate social networks were not directly oppositional, but in a mutually beneficial relationship to the governing system. I am not arguing that Czech bluegrassers were complicit in an overt way with the ruling system, but I do want to highlight the complicated relationships that shaped late communism, and which persist in the Czech collective memory. Archipelagoes of relationships such as those that link cottagers and bluegrassers created alternate discourses and relational practices that persist today.

PERFORMING BETWEENNESS, LOCATING IDENTITY

Yurchak (2006) provides greater nuance to Ash's cynical characterization of Czech collaboration. He examines elements by which Russians during "late socialism" (a period he sets in the 1970s–1980s that corresponds with the "normalization" era in Czechoslovakia) organized and rationalized their daily lives. I recount some of these elements here to indicate how cultural practices from the period of late socialism have shaped Czech Americanism.

Yurchak identifies elements of discourse in Russian life that have "constative" and "performative" natures. Constative speech is the simple saying of something, such as the sentence "It is cold." Performative language acts accomplish something in their articulation, such as the pronouncement of marriage or the naming of a ship.[24] In bluegrass discourse, some common performative statements include expressing (performatively) a preference for traditionalist bluegrass through singing "Blue Ridge Cabin Home" like Flatt and Scruggs instead of like the Bluegrass Album Band, or in the sort of nuanced performatives that formulate identifications based on location, origin, and social context that Bealle (1993) has noted in his study of US bluegrass festival stage talk.

Yurchak (2006, 117) argues that subjects of Russian "late socialism" did not vote yes in a *constative* response to the question, "Do you support the regime?" He argues that in that moment, citizens understood the vote as a *performative* act, implying the question, "Are you the kind of people who understand that the norms and rules of the current regime need to be performatively reproduced, that constative meanings do not necessarily have to be attended to, who act accordingly, and who, therefore, can be engaged in other meanings?" (ibid.). The idea that subjects of a repressive communist regime would have implicit permission to engage in projects that create other meanings allows us to see Czech Americanism in a space between dissent and complicity.

Yurchak's discussion of "deterritorialization" is even more pertinent, as it places this process in the real and imagined spaces of late socialist life.[25] He argues that there is no single Soviet public sphere, but "a process of deterritorialization in which multiple deterritorialized publics, not static public spheres, were continuously produced" (2006, 118). This sort of identification with community rings true in my observation of Czech bluegrass practice today, which often involves this sort of flexible participation in social groups as well as in musical styles.

The roots of this sort of flexibility have deeper political significance, as we see in one of Yurchak's examples. A government employee named Inna describes how she would not resist in an active or subversive way the authoritative discourse that suffused life in the Soviet Union. Instead of dissident protests such as Václav Havel's (1989) emphasis on "living in truth" and Solzhenitsyn's (2004) appeal "to live not by lies," Inna and her friends spoke of "'living lightly' . . . 'leading a very fun life' . . . and 'making merry in general,'" not to declare the nonseriousness of existence, but as an act of replacing Soviet political and social concerns with "a quite different set of concerns that allowed one to lead a creative and imaginative life" (Yurchak 2006, 132). In this mindset and social situation, bluegrass music making could serve as a form of "emigration from the constative dimension of authoritative discourse, but not from all meanings and realities of socialist life" (133).

Yurchak finds that many Russians in this period not only qualified their discursive position in society as marginal to official discourse; they often regarded their location itself to be multivocal, multisited, and in flux (19). When some Russian writers refer to "being *vnye*," they don't mean only the literal notion of "inside," but rather a condition of in-betweenness that Yurchak finds to be intrinsic to life in the "deterritorialized milieus" of late socialist Russia. Drawing on the writings of literary theorist Mikhail Bakhtin (1990, 2004), Yurchak argues that the term refers to *vnyenakhodimost*, "inside/outside-locatedness," emphasizing a relationship between inside and outside (133). To be *vnye* was thus to live within the daily life of late socialism, and to take a position to comment on that life.

Czech Americanisms display at every turn the sort of dialogic engagement Yurchak describes. Czech bluegrassers embody the ambiguity of *vnye* in their fluid conception of location and identity: they are inside/outside America as they are inside/outside their Czech identity and Central European location. Bluegrass music, already deterritorialized from its putative origins in the horse-raising country of Kentucky to its commercial commodification through the late twentieth century, lends itself to reterritorialization—in ways similar to other Americanisms, like Western films and the cowboy image.

HEARING RETERRITORIALIZATION

At the beginning of my fieldwork, I still heard echoes of this play with territories in the songs that were created by Czech bluegrassers during the late socialist period. One particularly memory-filled and resonant space for me was U Supa, the western-themed pub I describe in chapter 1. I have attended bluegrass jams at U Supa since 2002, at which point it seemed an island of "old Prague," still undeveloped by the real estate projects and the EU-supported grants that would eventually gentrify many parts the city.

When I brought out my fiddle and sat down at the jam table on my first visit to U Supa, I was immersed in songs familiar from bluegrass jams and performances at home—all retexted and reterritorialized for use in this situation. Zdeněk, a tram driver for Prague's transportation authority, quickly oriented

The table in U Supa where the author attended bluegrass jams during 2002–2003 and 2007–2008 on Tuesday and Thursday nights, 2016.

me, and helped me order a beer (an important part of jam participation—Věra Kubíková, the bass player, would give me a number of beer-etiquette lessons in my visits to the jam in ensuing years).

Zdeněk always sat at the pub table with a fat three-ring binder open amid the beer glasses in front of him, leading the singing and playing. A holdover from the pre-internet world, this collection of texts represented years of collecting and editing—a trove of information useful for keeping the fun of the jam going. As the group would go from song to song, Zdeněk thus held a position of authority and prominence. He would clue me in to the original English title and composer of each song, often opening a discussion of important recorded performances of it by Czech and US artists, a liminal space indicating the transcultural mixing of bluegrass with Czech practices.

The Czech texts that this and many other groups use were the output of early bands such as the Greenhorns, White Stars, and Rangers, and of star singer Pavel Bobek and others who were the first to encounter and reproduce American country and bluegrass in the 1960s and 1970s. These are the "oldies" or "classics" of the Czech bluegrass world. In the several generations of musical transmission since these songs were hot pop commodities, they (and their texts) have been widely disseminated throughout Czech musical life. One song that I was particularly struck by in 2002–2003 was "Myslím na Colorado"

(I'm thinking of Colorado), a retexting by the venerable Plzeň-based band Cop (Ponytail) of the Bill Monroe/Chuck Carson classic "Cheap Love Affair" (Rosenberg and Wolfe 2007, 126). The song, which I heard countless times at U Supa, allows Czechs to sing with reference to iconic Americana: the place of Colorado (pronounced, following Cop frontman Míša Leicht's lead, as "Colorejdo") and the sound of the "blues."

The playful articulation of imagined Americanness in this and many other songs can inspire communal singing not only from the musicians around the jam table, but from individuals who are part of the normal crowd at the bar or the table football machine. The world created in English bluegrass lyrics is one that evokes nostalgic longing with its seemingly timeless landmarks like "mother," "home," and other rooted and rooting entities. The universality of these tropes and the extent to which they were a part of popular culture in the 1970s–1990s might explain the persistence of these songs in the Czech popular consciousness through normalization and after 1989.

Another song that I remember hearing during those Tuesday jams shows how musical practices from past decades engaged in deterritorialization in creating meaning in between states and places. The song was all about bluegrass music itself—or, as I realized as my Czech language skills improved, all about an idealized vision of the music as it existed in the American landscape:

Bluegrass/Modrá tráva

VERSE 1: Once while hanging around in Tennessee, I first heard that banjo play.
Music so driving, yet beautiful, that I just had to laugh.

CHORUS: Now, that is really bluegrass, only bluegrass sounds that way.
On the wide open plains, bluegrass is waving. Now, that is Tennessee.

VERSE 2: Every cowboy and farmer who lives in Tennessee loves this music.
And that is why all of them, old and young, know how to play it well.

VERSE 3: Guitar and banjo, harmonica and bass, whatever is at hand.
The hard-driving fiddle has a place in the band, and the mandolin as well.

VERSE 4: Because of this music, I have thrown away my rambling shoes.
I have stayed for good in the land of this music, I have stayed right here in Tennessee.[26]

While searching for the author of this song, I learned that many people have heard it, in different forms, in different places—and with differing reactions.[27] I also sense a bit of ambivalence from some younger musicians about its text, which they consider to be over the top, and clearly incongruent with the actual United States. At the threshold between the 1980s and 1990s, a variety of changes allowed Czechs to access information about the West, and about the actual places, sounds, and people of American bluegrass.

THE END OF THE 1980S—AND OF COMMUNISM

The maturation of bluegrass-related musicking in the 1970s and 1980s and the social situations of normalization solidified the importance of this form of recreation in Czech society, and formed the particular negotiation between imagination and reality that it afforded participants. Both in the (increasingly media-dominated) mainstream and also in private, small-scale efforts, bluegrass musical elements became a deeply rooted part of Czech life. Many of the Czech bluegrass players I encountered in my field research date their first encounters with the music to this period.

The life story of Prague fiddler František "Franta" Kacafírek, as he related it to me in a number of interviews in the spring of 2008, offers some perspective on the final decades of the communist period and the transition to the present way of life in the Czech Republic. I focus on his playing and views more in the following chapter, but introduce him here so that I can also introduce some significant groups from his heyday during "late communism."

Kacafírek first heard bluegrass-related music from the Greenhorns, and was captivated by the fiddling of Petr Bryndač. After quitting his state-mandated training as a machinist in the early 1970s, he took up the fiddle and—in a rare move for a bluegrass community that in the main is supported by members' day jobs—has worked almost exclusively as a fiddler and violinist ever since. Franta played with many groups in his early days as a musician, including Zvonky (Bells), Old Friends, and Křupani (Hillbillies), before being selected himself to play with the Greenhorns, or as they were known at that time, Zelenáči. As part of this group at the peak of their popular success (the mid-1970s through the mid-1980s), Kacafírek traveled to West Germany to play at the Karl May Festspiele and to other foreign locales in addition to touring around Czechoslovakia.

Younger than Čermák and the founding members of the Greenhorns, Franta gravitated toward the next generation of players, notably another Prague musician, Petr Kůs. A gifted singer and lyricist and skilled mandolinist, Kůs led the group Poutníci Praha (Pilgrims Prague), which later became better known under the name Blanket. Franta's fiddling was a key part of the group's performances, but the smoothly modulated vocals of Kůs, guitarist and tenor singer Milan Menda, and bass player and singer Antonis

Strana A

1.	DURHAM'S REEL / tradicional	2´11˝
2.	ŘEKNI HVĚZDÁM / M. Menda, P. Kůs	2´53˝
3.	PRVNÍ PŮJDU DÁL / CLIMBING UP THE MOUTAIN / tradicional / P. Kůs	1´52˝
4.	PROUD PEŘEJÍ / M.Menda, P. Kůs	2´57˝
5.	ZEM MODRAVEJCH PLÁNÍ / P. Kůs	2´36˝
6.	MOU ZPRÁVU DEJTE LIDEM / GET DOWN BROTHER / S. Ludlam, P. Kůs	2´39˝
7.	SWEET GEORGIA BROWN / B. Bernie, H. Pinkard, K. Casey	4´22˝

Strana B

8.	HÁDKA S ANDĚLEM / MY LORD HEARD JERUSALEM WHEN SHE MOANED / tradicional / P. Kůs	2´21˝
9.	OTEVŘI DVEŘE DOKOŘÁN / WHATAMI DOING MANGING AROUND / Lewis, Clarke, J. Lebeda	2´28˝
10.	VYPLOUVÁM / TOP OF THE WORLD / tradicional / P. Kůs	2´58˝
11.	JSEM TULÁK JEN / FREE BORN MAN / K. Allison, M. Lindsay / P. Kůs	3´04˝
12.	KENTUCKY WALTZ / B. Monroe / M. Šlambora	2´54˝
13.	BLEEKER STREET RAG / Randy Scruggs	3´40˝

Liner notes for Blanket's Bluegrass *album (Apollo, 1991) show that tracks 3, 6, and 8 are gospel songs translated by Petr Kůs. Author's collection.*

Timiopulos also added to the band's popularity. Kůs retexted numerous bluegrass classics with Czech lyrics, focusing especially on gospel songs, which until then had been largely left out of Czech bluegrass-related music making. Kůs's take on the bluegrass and southern gospel classic "On the Sea of Life" echos Doyle Lawson's take on the song, with soaring tenor vocals over the chugging bass and lead lines that create a compelling vocal harmony sound. Blanket's version of the song "Ashes of Love" (retexted as "Z lásky jen dým") shows that they were working in parallel with the US bluegrass vogue at the time, in which the sophisticated musical sensibility and polished, high-pitched vocality of performers like the Osborne Brothers, Doyle Lawson, and Joe Val were at the forefront of bluegrass popularity.

Another band named Poutníci was formed in Brno in the 1970s. Brno, the second-largest city in the current Czech Republic, has long served as an important center of culture, government, and education. A short distance from Vienna, it is located in the middle of the Moravia region, with its distinctive wine culture and vibrant music and dance traditions, and so its bluegrass scene has always been a bit different from the bluegrass-related activity in Bohemia, which centered around Prague.

Robert Křesťan, the singer and lyricist of Poutníci Brno, was key to the band's success. Křesťan, a literary translator for English-writing authors, is known widely for his artful translation of English song texts, his composition of new Czech texts for existing American bluegrass melodies (as well, for example, as the songs of Bob Dylan and Irish traditional songs), and his original Czech-language compositions. Křesťan's role as an interpreter of literature and song texts is apt. One of the Czech equivalents for the English word performer is *interpret*, a linguistic "false friend" that highlights the importance of translation in the act of performance.

Czech musicians who, like Křesťan, compose their own song texts are highly valued in the Czech folk scene, as it is largely based on the singer-songwriter model of American postwar folk music, which includes the work of artists such as Joan Baez and Bob Dylan. Czechs' literary interest and high literacy are often cited in common discourse as contributing to the refined sense of culture that is part of the Czech national image (Holý 1996).

The songs that Křesťan interpreted while he was with this group remain in the collective memory as classics not only of the Czech bluegrass scene, but also among folk audiences and wider circles of Czech society. The group was also distinguished musically, featuring a spectacular instrumental lineup with virtuosic banjo work by Luboš Malina. In its earliest incarnations, the band also included musicologist, folklore expert, and mandolinist Jiří Plocek, who contributed to the group's popular and sophisticated arrangements of traditional dance tunes taken from the work of Czech composers such as Bedřich Smetana.

Robert Křesťan and Poutníci, ca. 1990. Photo by Lilly Pavlak, used with permission.

Along with the work of Poutníci and other bands of their generation, festivals continued to flourish through the 1980s, fostering ongoing interest in the music. Bluegrass-related activity and interest continued to deepen both in the aging echelon of "first-generation" bluegrassers and in the younger waves of interested Czechs who were "hooked" by hearing older players. In a move that can be read both as a loosening of restrictions and as part of a plan of appeasement, the government allowed tours of bluegrass musicians previously inaccessible (in local performance, at least) to Czech audiences—Mark O'Connor and Byron Berline's visits in the 1980s and 1990s are remembered in legendary terms by older Czech bluegrassers.

AFTER 1989

According to Helena Pavličíková (2000, 120), "November 1989 marked the end of one chapter of the history of Czech folk music. Czech folk music is now in an entirely different situation than the situation that prevailed practically during the entire period of its development in this country." The dividing line of 1989 as denoting the "end of communism" and the "beginning of democracy," however, is often fuzzier and more complicated than scholars like Pavličíková make it out to be. The past was not erased by the governmental and economic changes of the early 1990s, and the postsocialist world has in some ways not proved to be all that different from the one that preceded it. Some outsiders' views of the "revolutions" that transformed the Eastern Bloc in 1989–1991 treat the situation as if the big problem was solved in 1989, and as if an open and democratic future would change the way life happened in formerly communist Eastern Europe. However, the complex terrain of postsocialism often ends up being as focused on the past as it is on the future.

Alexei Yurchak has emphasized the importance of examining larger arcs of history in considering postsocialism. In his study of the naming of businesses by post-1991 Russian entrepreneurs, Yurchak (2000, 419) finds that the conventions of naming were neither simply reactions to the communist legacy nor entirely new creations. In a surprising move, he finds some roots for the current business-naming models (such as acronyms and name agglomerations) in Russian experimental revolutionary culture of the 1910s and '20s and its quest for a new "transrational language."

In considering the phenomenon of Czech cottaging after 1989, Reidinger (2007, 40) also takes a longer view, considering "pre-socialism" as an important influence on the unfolding era after communism. Reidinger implies an important question: Why, then, did cottaging, as well as other Americanist recreations, still happen after 1989—is this just "a 'hangover' from communism" (40)? One problem in considering this question, Reidinger proposes, is that "most Western democratic theory does not predict or account for the intense dissatisfaction, or, rather more frequently, outright and explicit disgust with political processes and those who occupy public office that is typical for Czechs all across their political spectrum," as manifested in voting records: "In some elections, as few as 3% of eligible voters turn out to cast their ballots." Politics, she continues pessimistically, is not the only target of dissatisfaction with communal action: "In this country, Scouts are the subjects of tasteless jokes, church attendance is extremely low in most regions, and in many areas, only very old women attend church, where they are served by Polish and other foreign priests—because the Church is unable to recruit young Czech men. Furthermore, church leaders lament that the combination of the two-day weekend with cottaging has undermined believers' church attendance, as they may elect to spend the time with their families in areas that lack a church" (41–42).

Recreation and re-creation as alternatives to the place and regime of "daily life" have extended past the communist period into the present, along with the implicit complicity of Czechs with a government intent on controlling dissent. Reidinger (2007, 42) relates how many Czechs continue to avoid politically sensitive urban situations through retreat: "[T]he socialist regime often recommended that people go and winterize their country homes or plant potatoes whenever some demonstration or other public nuisance was in the works. The current state also makes such explicit recommendations in times of impending crisis. For example, the government, through various media, encouraged people to depart Prague for their cottages before the 2000 World Bank/International Monetary Fund summit (during which there were great riots), and again, and even more emphatically before the 2001 NATO summit."

Other continuities persist as well. Geographer Petr Jehlicka's historical and sociological investigation (Jehlicka 2008; Jehlicka and Smith 2007) reveals the importance of Americanists' appreciation of nature as one of the most significant motivations for environmentalist efforts in the Czech lands, through the twentieth century and today. In recent research with members of the environmental movement, Jehlicka (2008, 128) found that more than half of his respondents cited "woodcraft-inspired culture" (such as books by E. T. Seton and Karl May, and experiences with tramping or scouting) as the "formative experience" and inspiration for their environmentalist efforts.

NOSTALGIA AND THE GOOD/BAD OLD DAYS

Repertory and styles of early, communist-era Czech bluegrass still thrive, mostly in the rural margins and among older generations, but most younger bluegrassers follow groups like Reliéf into more cosmopolitan realms. Thus I was surprised in 2008 to learn of the band Kojoti (the Coyotes). The members of Kojoti are student-aged Prague musicians who have chosen *not* to employ their generation's refined training in English and enhanced access to media to copy American groups and sounds. Instead they turn inward, performing material taken from Czech bluegrass originators like White Stars, Bobři, and the Greenhorns.

The late twentieth-century fads of German "Ostalgie" and "Yugomania" (Hofman 2009) show that Czechs are not alone in their nostalgia for the old days, with their mix of good and bad. The particular way in which this nostalgia is articulated reveals some steps in the complicated dance both between past and present and between Czech and American. Another Prague band, Sunny Side, released an album in 2002 entitled *Staří Greenhorni*, a tribute to the classic songs made famous by the Greenhorns. Like Kojoti, Sunny Side have modified the typical appropriation process of Czech bluegrass, drawing from the local Czech past instead of from the United States.

Perhaps because the members of Sunny Side are older, their historically oriented project is more nuanced. Consider, for instance, the title of their cover album. In identifying the object of their tribute, Sunny Side did not use the original English-language band name (the Greenhorns) or the Czech alternative (Zelenáči). Instead, they "Czechified" the venerable band's English name, adding the Czech male animate plural ending appropriate for the terminal *n* sound to produce a mixed English-Czech nonword, " Greenhorni." The members of Sunny Side typically take pride in their mastery of English, singing traditional bluegrass in its original language. With this album title, though, they use Czech grammar in a performative localization of the English word in a way that simultaneously distances them from and grounds them in their particularly Czech tradition.

In 2007 I returned to Kozlová Stodola (the site of the Lhotka workshop that I describe at the beginning of chapter 1) to play a festival with the band Roll's Boys. If I squint the eyes of my memory, the weekend could have taken place twenty, thirty, or forty years ago: The festival was held in a fixed-up barn in a secluded rural area far from a large city and mass transit routes. Folks gathered to play bluegrass—sung in English and Czech, on stage and off. A hat was passed to help the bands pay for gas. Nobody's mobile phone worked, and all those speedy Czech SMS-typing fingers were stilled, or redirected to late-night jamming around the woodstove. The bar tab was kept the old way, with rows of pencil marks tallied on small sheets of white paper.

When my energy gave out, I left the jam circle to sleep a bit of Saturday night—technically it was Sunday morning—in my sleeping bag in a smelly room, stacked with other tired bluegrassers into the rows of army surplus bunks that had been shoved together to maximize space. In the morning, before heading home, we divvied up the remaining pickled sausages and beer left over from the previous night's fun.

It all seemed fairly natural to me until I was offered a ride back to Prague by a friend. I tossed my bag and fiddle in the back and buckled my seatbelt. As we sat for a few minutes while the group in front of us wrestled their aging Škoda out of a rut in the muddy driveway, I realized how odd it was, after this weekend out of time, to suddenly be back in 2007, in a minivan with the mainstream station Evropa 2 pumping global pop out of the stereo. For in all the contradictions involved, the people who make Czech bluegrass—and my work to understand and write about what they are doing—are part of reckoning not only with the present and the foreign, but also with the familiar and the past.

3

MAKING BLUEGRASS AT HOME, ABROAD, AND IN BETWEEN

TOURING EUROPE WITH ROLL'S BOYS

When I met Zdeněk Roh and the band Roll's Boys at the Berlin airport on May 17, 2006, it marked the beginning of that summer's "field" adventure. I've gotten used to the "in-between" of air transit and airports, and the blur of the world as I am in the process of flying from the New World to the Old. In the course of my many trips to and from the Czech Republic, the dozen or so hours of air travel and the cultural adjustments have become fairly routine.

This trip was unusual in that I was meeting with Czech bluegrassers not on their home turf but in a country foreign to both of us. Due to cost cutting and some ambitious trip planning on my part, I was flying in to meet Roll's Boys halfway through their 1,000-kilometer drive from Jihlava in the Czech Republic to Fredericia, Denmark. I am still amazed that on that gray day in Germany I was able to find the band in the parking lot, and that the unlikely plan I had helped hatch months before was actually going to work. Just minutes after I rolled off the plane and trundled groggily through customs, I greeted Zdeněk in the concourse and was ushered into a borrowed red minivan for another seven hours of travel. We spent the rest of the day driving up to the Bruunske Pakhus, the venue in Fredericia where we were booked to perform for the weekend. This road trip with Roll's Boys was about the same as the trip I had made with them in 2005 to the Akusztikus Zenei Fesztivál in Abaliget, Hungary, and far shorter than our 2004 trip to

Roll's Boys and van on the road to Norway, 2004.

the Countryfestivalen Skjåk in Norway. Our epic 2004 trip included thirty hours of driving, a ride on a North Sea ferry that we barely caught, and my harrowing first experience with driving on the German Autobahn.

The "in-between" space of a band's road travel from one engagement to the next is a storied one, especially in the United States, and for bluegrass musicians. Ralph Stanley recalls harrowing and humorous tales from his days traveling with his brother between stints on radio stations throughout the urban eastern seaboard and at schoolhouses and other rural venues (Stanley and Dean 2009). Road stories from sidemen who worked with Bill Monroe abound, including cross-country drives that rival the trips I took with Roll's Boys (Black 2005, 31–35; Rosenberg and Wolfe 2007, 150). Our road-trip experiences all contain many similar elements: confinement, camaraderie, and monotony punctuated by moments of transcendent performance in which the community of the band members who travel by car is shared with the audience they have traveled so long to meet.

Soon after we arrived, we took the stage and played our fifty-minute set in the Friday night show that opened the festival. The band was well received in spite of the jet-lagged state of their American fiddler, whose adrenalin store had just about been exhausted—by the time we took the stage, I had been on the go and without sleep for almost twenty-seven hours. The virtuosic instrumental performances of Ralph Schut on guitar, Eda Krištůfek on mandolin, and Zdeněk Roh on banjo were highlights.

Still, although we were met with warm applause, the Danish crowd didn't seem overwhelmed by the Czechs' performance. My experiences taking part in and observing concerts with Roll's Boys and other Czech bluegrass groups in other European countries have given me a perspective on reception in the European bluegrass scene at large. At the 2004 festival in Norway, the 2005 Akusztikus Festival in Hungary, and the European Bluegrass Music Association's European World of Bluegrass Festival in Voorthuizen, Netherlands, in 2003, the group was much more enthusiastically praised for their

The author with Roll's Boys at the Nemzetközi Bluegrass és Akusztikus Zenei Fesztivál in Abaliget, Hungary, 2005.

skillful performance of bluegrass music. In Hungary and Norway, bluegrass is not as naturalized and polished as it is in the Czech Republic, and at the European World of Bluegrass festival, Czechs (and Slovaks) generally make up about half of the several dozen bands who perform, making them a sort of "home team" plurality in that scene, one in which Roll's Boys have held a distinguished position.

The difference in reception in Fredericia was likely due to a number of details about this festival. I would argue that it also indicates the role of Czech bluegrass performers in the regional European scene. Roll's Boys were not a premier entry in the Fredericia lineup; they were warming up the stage for the headliner, Valerie Smith, and her band, Liberty Pike. The significance of the American groups (aesthetic, cultural, and economic) was greater than that accorded to the (mostly) Czech makeup of our delegation. As a band we were, like the (more) local Scandinavian groups who kicked off the evening's show, a European imitation of Valerie Smith's American performance of the music.

This hierarchy was mirrored in the billing and performance order for that evening in Fredericia: local band, then regional band, then the major star—a system used by bluegrass and country music promoters since the mid-1900s (Rosenberg 2005, 155). Within the European bluegrass scene, which struggles with concerns about imitation and creativity (such as the issues of "self-expression" and improvisation I discuss in chapter 4), Czech bluegrassers occupy a special position as regional favorites.

Czechs are well paid to perform all over Europe, especially in the wealthier northern and western countries, and are often mentioned both in Europe and in the United States as one of the best sources of bluegrass interest and expertise outside the southern US. European event organizers and festival promoters who hire them don't have to pay transatlantic airfare, but can still provide a well-produced performance of bluegrass music at their events. Czechs often serve in a transitional role between local groups (such as the Swedish and Danish groups at the Fredericia event) and American players. As they travel and perform around their home region, Czech bluegrass players and their performance are active in a space "between" European scenes and the United States.

For Czech musicians, this transitional status is often advantageous. For one thing, financial and time constraints make it difficult for most Czech bluegrassers to travel to play in the United States. In marketing their performance of Americanness in the wealthier countries of Europe, they support their activities financially, augment their prestige both at home and abroad, and have the opportunity to meet, hear, and often play with the stars of the American scene.

PLAYING TRANSITIONS

Traveling with Roll's Boys is often hectic, with tight driving schedules resulting from members' inflexible workweeks bookending a weekend event. Still, we take as many chances as we can to enjoy our time "abroad." I am a foreigner twice over when I travel with the band. This role can be helpful, as I can offer fluent English when the Czech natives have trouble understanding the English spoken by a Hungarian waiter or an inebriated Norwegian bartender. More often, though, I feel like I am just a part of the Czech delegation that our band becomes at bluegrass events. I first felt this way during our trip to Norway in 2004, where all of us in the group were already a bit delirious from being in the car, disoriented by the never-ending daylight of the near-arctic latitude, and astounded by the extreme inebriation of the Norwegian festival-goers.

We would walk from our cabin near the festival site across the grounds to the side stage where we performed, and stare unabashedly at figures dressed from head to toe in black leather chaps, duster coats, spurs, and the ubiquitous black Stetson-style cowboy hats who were struggling to stay upright, or brawling in the mud that developed on footpaths over the course of the weekend event. I am not in the same alcohol-consumption league as many of my Czech colleagues, but the members of Roll's Boys are definitely no lightweights when it comes to drinking. Still, we all spoke in hushed tones in Czech among ourselves, wondering about the Norwegian national character and festival traditions, which appeared to us to be based in a near-toxic intake of hard liquor.[1]

In Fredericia, our band was a similarly separate group, but in less bizarre surroundings that allowed me to more fully observe my Czech colleagues' reactions to other performers. Lodged in a "folk school" (a remodeled monastery) overlooking a sea channel, we met a number of interesting local and visiting performers, and had more time for relaxation than is usual on a tour. In addition to seeing some of the sights of the town, we enjoyed the other acts at the festival. On Saturday, our Czech-American Roll's Boys group was off duty, so we hung out in the pub and talked, for the most part ignoring a set by the Abrams Brothers, a pair of adolescent up-and-coming Canadians. While the Boys were impressed by the instrumental chops of the brothers' backing band, the sounds coming from the stage weren't reason enough to leave the vicinity of the beer tap. As that group left the stage, though, Zdeněk initiated a move into the performance space to get seats up front for the set by Valerie Smith and her headlining band. I enjoyed watching both Friday and Saturday nights' shows from the first row—noticing that my Czech colleagues displayed a rapt attention to the stage, punctuated only by enthusiastic

Western dancers on the main stage at the Country Festivalen in Skjåk, Norway, 2004.

applause and excited comments to each other that glowed with appreciation and approval.

The reverence with which my Czech friends attended to the younger musicians (including fiddler Becky Buller) that Valerie Smith had brought as her backing band was a technical appreciation. The band backed Smith with soul and precision, and offered up some solo performances that were top-notch. We were also tickled to see Richard Ciferský included in this group. Richard had been drafted as the banjo player for the band's European tour, replacing Smith's usual banjoist.

Richard is known in his native Slovakia as well as in the United States for his work with the Czech/Slovak band Fragment. Fragment's frequent US tours have spread both a familiarity with the band itself and an appreciation for the phenomenon of Czech (and Slovak) bluegrass. Richard's role as a "ringer" is the opposite of the situation I usually find myself in—as the sole American with a Czech group. Besides saving the band the cost of another transatlantic air ticket, and adding another strong player to their sound, Richard's presence brought some "local" knowledge and language ability that helped Valerie and the band navigate around Europe.

Both for Czechs performing elsewhere in Europe as representatives of the Czech bluegrass scene and for those embedded within an "American" tour, "being bluegrass" necessitates many experiences and negotiations of "in-betweenness." Ciferský has many stories similar to mine, and to the ones that I share with Roll's Boys—about the Americans he traveled, worked, and had fun with in the summer of 2006, plus many more about his numerous trips to other locations in other bluegrass situations. I particularly enjoy the story about our meeting on the Fourth of July in 2005, when Fragment played in a bookstore venue in downtown Charlottesville, Virginia. My story centers on the mix of familiarity and foreignness I felt as I experienced Czech bluegrass in the town where I lived (and in which I was conducting graduate studies). His story of the event reveals a parallel mixture: Richard and the other band members recall being surprised to discover someone in a smallish Virginia city who could converse with them in Czech and was conducting research on what they were doing.

HANDCRAFTING "AMERICA" IN THE CZECH REPUBLIC

Apart from tours by bands like Fragment, the most tangible presence of the Czech bluegrass community in the United States is also the most successful commercial Czech bluegrass product: bluegrass-related musical instruments. For a period of time in the early twenty-first century, Gibson instruments contained a few pounds of Czech-made metal parts manufactured by Jaroslav Průcha, Laďa Ptáček, and Pavel Krištůfek. These three craftsmen have supplied banjo parts for many major US banjo builders, and widely market high-quality reproductions of vintage parts for upgrading existing instruments. Their production of banjos and parts is more than just an expansion of the United States–based bluegrass industry; it reflects an outgrowth of the Czech bluegrass "transition," a new way that Czechs have found to "be bluegrass" for fun, but also for profit.

In addition to introducing Czechs to the form and function of the five-string banjo, Pete Seeger's Czech performances in 1964 helped translate this foreign instrument into Czech musical and lutherie practice. In the live recording made at his Prague concert that year, Seeger (2001) congenially announces his presence (in Czech), and then tears through a hot version of the Jimmie Rodgers classic "T for Texas." As many who heard this momentous performance (either live or via radio or recordings) continue to attest, it was an amazing experience to hear those notes, the bouncing, churning stream of rhythmic figures that poured from Seeger's hands and instrument. I should make it clear that Seeger's introductory banjo fanfare is not "bluegrass" playing, the three-finger "roll" technique made famous by Earl Scruggs in his tenure as one of Bill Monroe's Blue Grass Boys in the 1940s and '50s. Neither was the instrument Seeger played a "bluegrass" banjo. It was an instrument made specially for him by the Vega company, with an extended neck that allowed him to play in tunings that suited his singing voice, and without a resonator covering the back, both characteristics that distinguished it from the standard five-string banjos played by Earl Scruggs, Don Reno, Bill Keith, and others who have shaped the role of the banjo in bluegrass.

Despite its quirks, Seeger's banjo was an instrument that could be used to play music that referenced bluegrass, this music that somehow had captured the imaginations of these Czech folks. Marko Čermák, the pioneer of Czech bluegrass-style banjo, is famously credited with reconstructing a facsimile of Seeger's instrument from photographs taken at the concert, and then studiously applying himself to learning the Scruggs style of playing. As I describe in chapter 2, Čermák eventually procured a proper bluegrass-type instrument, and the Czech banjos and banjoists that succeeded him have continued to more closely resemble their US bluegrass ideal.

Jaroslav Průcha is part of the next generation of banjo makers who, inspired by Čermák's ingenuity, continued and improved upon his banjo-making work. In 1978 Průcha moved from amateur building to the professional production of banjos for other Czechs eager to participate in the bluegrass phenomenon. In a conversation in 2003 at his booth at the annual Banjo Jamboree festival in Kopidlno, he told me about a visit he made to Nashville in the mid-1980s to see the Gibson Company's banjo-manufacturing facility. He didn't fully explain how he was able to make this trip—few Czechs were able to travel to the "West" during this period. Thus Průcha's presence at that time in that place was doubly exceptional: Gibson instruments, particularly mandolins and banjos, are almost inextricable from style itself. Průcha had arrived, in some ways, at the heart of the American bluegrass banjo universe.

While visiting Gibson, Průcha perceived an opportunity. The banjo parts that, because of trade restrictions, he had been forced to make himself rather than import could be profitably marketed in the United States. After 1989's "Velvet Revolution," he was able to approach Gibson about providing metal

*Průcha banjos, old (**left**) and new (**right**), showing the progress this maker has made in his inlay and finish work. From Vladimír Mazálek's collection at his Banjo Eden* museum *in Bojkovice, Czech Republic, 2009.*

banjo parts for their instruments. While Gibson would not confirm the information when I contacted them several times over more than a decade, Průcha told me that he has supplied products not only for Gibson, but for many other US banjo manufacturers as well, sharing the market with fellow Czech makers Ptáček and Krištůfek (Eda's brother Pavel). With the decline of Gibson's acoustic instrument production following the 2010 flooding in Nashville, Tennessee, Průcha has produced more of his own parts, marketing them through firms like Stewart-MacDonald and First Quality Music.

Průcha has also led other Czech makers into the international instrument market. Since the mid-1990s, banjos, mandolins, and guitars with names like Lebeda, Krishot, Holoubek, and Čapek on their pegheads have been appearing with more frequency in the United States and elsewhere outside the Czech Republic. US bluegrassers are eager to obtain these top-quality handmade instruments, which cost less than comparable American ones and have a unique cachet that mixes Old World mystique with bluegrass's down-home image. In a video review of his Holoubek mandolin, musician Lewin Barringer emphasizes that Ondra Holoubek is "a master luthier from the Czech Republic," whose "workmanship is top-notch. I can't tell you enough how many mandolin players—including Chris Thile—have played this mandolin and have been totally blown away, especially when you tell them how much you paid for it."[2] Czech instrument makers' competitive edge in the global market is sharpened by the economic history of the Czech Republic. As Průcha told me, "Everything here is cheaper." But the present success of Czech bluegrass products has a more significant cause than the forty-year economic depression of state socialism. Czechs are able to produce these instruments and engage in the process not simply because of economic advantage, but because they are part of the century-old legacy of hybridizing musicality and creative appropriation that I have outlined.

Younger Czechs whose experience of bluegrass has been formed by the post-1989 world are redefining this discourse to keep abreast of economic and social change. The dollar has lost roughly 40 percent of its value against the Czech crown since I first traveled to the Czech Republic in 2000. Where before Czech makers depended on American information and hard currency for survival of their craft, they now view the United States as just another part of their normal market. The post-2008 global economic situation finds the international bluegrass trade in roughly the same situation it was in before the recent crisis. While many in the business of bluegrass are experiencing a downturn along with a lot of other industries, there are still (as in the Great Depression and other economic hard times) Czech instrument makers who connect with customers interested in their work.

ZDENĚK ROH AND BANJOS IN BETWEEN

Like many younger Czech bluegrass players, Zdeněk Roh is a connoisseur of vintage 1950s and 1960s bluegrass, and relishes the classic records of Bill Monroe, Flatt and Scruggs, and others that are available in the era of democracy and the internet. He is also an expert on "prewar" Gibson Mastertone banjos, the holy grail for many bluegrass banjoists. His banjos are carefully crafted instruments that have a beefy low end and crisp highs that are sought after by bluegrass banjo players.

I have learned a lot about banjo making from Zdeněk, and I have observed how he markets his products—he has supplied instruments to dealers in the United States and the United Kingdom, and his products are in demand in the Czech Republic and elsewhere in Central Europe. The work he has done to craft a brand name for his banjos is an indication of their—and *his*—transitional situation. Like Průcha, Holoubek, and many other instrument makers in the Czech Republic, the United States, and elsewhere, Zdeněk decided to use his name as his brand identification. In keeping with his affinity for wordplay and his transcultural ken, he uses a version of his name that has undergone a series of significant transformations.

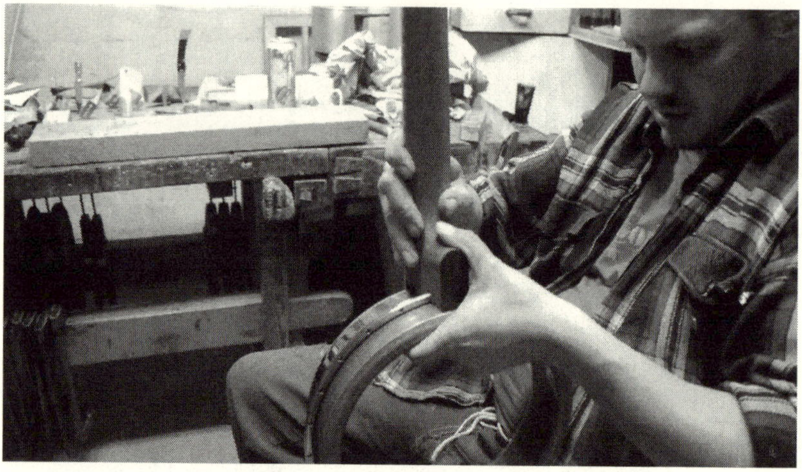

Zdeněk Roh in his workshop, Cerekvička, Czech Republic, 2013.

Not long after I met him in 2003, Zdeněk asked me my opinion of his brand name. He was very concerned about what I, as an American, thought about the name he had chosen to display on the headstocks of his instruments: "Roll's Banjos." As an American in the Czech bluegrass community, I have often been asked by Czechs to address not just grammatical uncertainties, but larger pragmatic issues. I am often asked by Czechs, for example, whether their newly composed English song lyrics "make sense" to a native speaker or whether an idiom is being used correctly, and to settle questions such as "Do Americans really all eat hamburgers for every meal?" and "Does everyone there play bluegrass?"

Picking apart the multiple layers of significance in Zdeněk's brand name reveals his care in crafting an image as well as the nature of the intercultural space in which he works as a craftsperson. Zdeněk's family name, Roh (which means "horn" or "corner"), led phonemically to his nickname, Rohlík, a diminutive that is also the name of the elongated crescent roll that is one of the most common foods in the Czech Republic. The English translation of his nickname, "roll," thus has no literal, daily-life use in the Czech context—but it shows his linguistic faculty and resonates with banjo players and their world. Banjoists who are reading this will know that the "roll" is the basic element of the right-hand banjo-picking technique made famous by Earl Scruggs, a technique that is central to the distinctive bluegrass sound. After Zdeněk explained this whole situation to me, his wife, Zdeňka, a teacher of British English, added that she appreciates how the name evokes the honed mechanical polish of Rolls-Royce automobiles.

The deft negotiation of meaning, prestige, and humor in this name indicates the interstitial location that Czech bluegrassers like Zdeněk occupy in creating their musical materials. Zdeněk is working to satisfy both the Americanist interests of Czech banjo players and the demands of buyers in the United States and elsewhere. His instruments themselves are linked to a specific locality, but are also similarly globalized. Zdeněk harvests wood from trees in his neighborhood that are both native to Czech soil and useful as tonewoods—he usually has a large stack at his workshop, aging until it is ready to be cut into banjo necks and other parts. Nearly all the metal parts he uses are Czech-made (by Průcha, Ptáček, and Krištůfek, the same trio who are part of the US banjo market), but when I spoke with him, he had just discovered that the finely shaped mother-of-pearl "Roll's" logos he inlays into each peghead can be obtained most cheaply from a firm in California that uses computer-controlled material-shaping equipment.

In addition to drawing on the same high-tech resources that are becoming standard for instrument makers worldwide, including in the Czech Republic,[3] Zdeněk adds his own innovations—one of which is actually a revival of a much older technique. After finding a container of old "hide glue" in his

Roll's "Mucha" banjo, built by Zdeněk Roh for US banjoist Tony Trischka in 2013. Photographed at Trischka's home in 2014.

workshop and recalling his grandfather's lessons about older gluing practices, he began to use this type of organically derived solution instead of cheaper synthetic glues. Although animal glue requires special handling (it must be heated, a process that Zdeněk accomplishes with the small woodstove near his workbench), he finds that it enables sound waves to be transmitted more completely through the wooden parts—which is why this is the glue most often used for violins and other fine instruments.

Through his building and marketing techniques, Zdeněk infuses what is often called "America's instrument" with a Czechness that is both metaphorical and concrete.[4] At one point, as we were walking through the woods near his home during the winter of 2008, he stopped and pointed up to a large maple in the hedgerow between the road and an agricultural field, saying that the tree's branch pattern and girth would allow him to make at least three or four good banjos from it. In his assessment of the bluegrass value of the tree, Zdeněk was bringing together his connections to the bluegrass world, his business, and the culture—and even the physical landscape—in which he lives. This integration is not always easy, as I explain below in discussing Roh's evolving career as a professional luthier.

AIDING AND ABETTING

For Czech bluegrassers, there are practicalities that complicate the sort of cross-cultural engagement I describe throughout this volume. Although Czechs are now more able to engage in international travel and discourse than they were in previous decades, they still encounter many obstacles as they pursue their avocational or business interests related to the music across regional and international borders. While musical instruments bear physical traces that make them indicators and expressions of culture, this physicality also means that considerable work is required to construct and procure them in spite of the language, cultural, governmental, and economic barriers.

Marko Čermák's homemade banjo replica from the 1960s is often cited as an early example of the negotiation of these barriers, but Czech bluegrassers still encounter difficulties similar to those that Čermák encountered: a lack of knowledge about instruments and how to play them, and a lack of the monetary means to secure instruments and other items—sound and video recordings, printed materials, as well as strings, picks, capos, tuners, and other accessories. I am always eager to help my Czech colleagues cross and avoid obstacles to their musical projects, in hopes of repaying in some small way the debt I owe them for their hospitality and willingness to participate in my academic and documentary projects.

For instance, I have on several occasions helped Zdeněk obtain banjo-making materials and banjo parts that would otherwise have been impossible for him to get. One of the most prestigious bluegrass-related instrument supply businesses refused to ship Zdeněk some items he needed for an instrument, including a specific kind of tuning pegs and some binding (a specially shaped strip of material used to cover and protect the corner seams of instruments and other vulnerable areas). I agreed to help by receiving the shipment of items at my home address; I then repacked them and sent them to his home in the Czech Republic.

I found myself in a similar situation in the fall of 2010 when my friend and research colleague Tomáš Dvořák called (surprising me when I saw the 420 international prefix for Czech lines show up on my US phone) to ask if I would be willing to relay an old guitar that he was hoping to buy from a seller on the auction site eBay. He explained that he was interested in fixing up the old instrument. I eventually realized that Tomáš hoped to do this with more than one guitar. I became more cautious, as I had been at the beginning when Zdeněk asked me for the same sort of help. I looked up the customs regulations in the Czech Republic and in the United States, as well as US Postal Service regulations: I didn't want to do anything illegal, or be a party to customs violations or taxing schemes. At the same time, however, I was intensely aware of the help that Tomáš, Zdeněk, and others have given

Tomáš Dvořák and partially restored guitars in his apartment workshop, Prague, Czech Republic, 2016.

me, both in personal ways and in ways that have aided my research (and this entire project) immensely.

Tomáš reassured me by saying that he doesn't *kšeftovat* (make money) with his guitar repairs. Tomáš is a technician who calibrates spectroscopes and other lab equipment; he tinkers with these musical instruments just for fun. The boundary between the professional and the personal is important in this sort of interaction, as it might affect the rate of taxes and even the cost of postage. For Tomáš, the "professional-level" costs of transnational instrument collecting would be too high, but he can literally afford to do it "just for fun."

CULTURAL TRANSLATION

When Pete Seeger introduced himself to his Czech audience at his Prague concert in 1964, he did so with a surprise. He expressed regret that he would not be able to talk to them in Czech—in serviceable Czech: "Je mi lito, že nemohu k vam mluvit česky." After pausing for the joke to take effect, and for his listeners to laugh, he continued in English: "I hope the banjo needs no translation" (Seeger 2001).[5] While the idea of music as a "universal language" is problematic, as illustrated, for example, by the dramatic case of Maori and British musical misunderstandings described by Martin Lodge (2009), the case of bluegrass in the Czech Republic shows at least that musics *can* carry intelligible meanings in translated form, far from home. The banjo, as an artifact that emerged from a history of transition, misunderstanding, and outright horror in the transfer of African people and ideas to the Americas, is a perfect example of objects' ability to carry and contain meanings "in between." An archaic definition of "translate" describes a "move from one place or situation to another," especially for clergy or religious relics.[6] Czech bluegrass involves translations of artifacts such as the banjo, as well as transitions of people who move between different geographical areas and spheres of life to make music, have fun, and—sometimes—make a living.

Zdeněk Roh's success as a banjo maker assures me that it is possible for Czechs to navigate between the promises and perils of bluegrass musicking, finding fun *and* commercial success between a rock and a hard place—"spoiling" the fun and recreative aspects of music through too much work, and vocational or business failure through not enough. Zdeněk Roh is in transition not only between Czech and American, but in his growing role as a bluegrass businessman. He has played bluegrass (on banjo, bass, guitar, and mandolin) at a high level in the Czech Republic for more than a decade, and has been tinkering with building banjos for almost as long—but these activities were always a background to his studies at the University of Economics in Prague and his work as an accountant for his father's company.

For most of the time I have known him, Zdeněk has split his time between making banjos and playing gigs with a number of bands, and keeping the books for the family firm. While I haven't inquired into his earnings or wealth, it is clear that he has managed fairly well. In 2010 he was able to finally afford the time and money to visit the United States for the first time. He spent time with my family in North Carolina, and visited local festivals as well as the sights and sounds of Nashville, western national parks, and the bluegrass festival in Telluride, Colorado. We even played with a pickup group at a friend's wedding, which was a novelty for partygoers in rural piedmont North Carolina. When guests came to the bandstand to compliment us and asked where we were from, they were universally (and understandably) surprised to learn that this outstanding banjo player was from a small town in the Czech Republic. Zdeněk was featured in the film *Banjo Romantika*, which I coproduced with filmmaker Shara Lange; we were excited to include him in the festivities surrounding the film's premiere in 2013.

Through hosting Zdeněk, helping with logistics, and just being a general guide and interpreter, I finally had a chance to repay in part, in token, the vast hospitality that he and his family have shown me over all the years I

Zdeněk Roh and the author at the premiere of the film Banjo Romantika *in Nashville, Tennessee, 2013.*

have spent time in the Czech Republic. After I dropped Zdeněk off at the train station to begin his long journey home, I realized that the personal connections I have made with Czech bluegrassers are the most powerful example of intercultural understandings that I can offer. The proximity of person-to-person interaction would thus seem to offer Czechs more intimate and compelling opportunities for learning about US bluegrass than records, instructional videos, or the printed page have afforded them in the past.

Czechs have earned respect for their technical ability and their artistic expressivity, and are perceived among European bluegrassers and in the United States as part of a distinctive bluegrass culture. For both high-level players and makers—and for those in the Czech Republic who are just learning to play the fiddle—this in-between status can lead to mixed emotions, as they sometimes feel both excitement and ambivalence about the local and global value of their own bluegrass creations.

4

LEARNING AND PLAYING AMERICANNESS ON THE FIDDLE

"WHY THE FIDDLE?"

In August 2007 I was freshly returned to the Czech Republic for a year of music, interviews, and learning from Czech bluegrassers. On arrival I had phoned Zdeněk Roh. He immediately invited me to accompany his family on their yearly vacation trip to the Šumava mountains along the border with Germany, where we would share a rented cottage with a group of musician friends.

On our last evening at the cottage, Zbyněk Bureš (a multi-instrumentalist and the leader of the group Reliéf) asked me about the goal of my project. I explained that I was seeking to explain the value that Americanness has for today's Czechs, with some aspects of Czech bluegrass–related music making as the units of study (the fiddle, gospel music, and banjo making, for example). Our conversation that evening had ranged from Czech conceptions of Native Americans to Czech dreams about traveling to the United States, topics that underlined my assertion that Czechs are deeply concerned with Americanness, so this answer seemed to stick.

Pushing on a point he found troubling, Zbyněk asked, "Proč ty housle?" (Why the fiddle?) "Fiddlers are all bad here," he said. "Why not write about the banjo or something else that Czechs are good at?"[1] I had been thinking that Czech fiddlers did not seem as accomplished (in technical skill or in expressive musicality) as their banjo-playing and mandolin-picking compatriots. Even as I expressed this critical view, I was cautious as I slipped into a common bluegrasser (insider) stance, one in which I compare live performances with recorded ones and perpetuate the cycles of evaluative listening that underlie Czech bluegrass. Still, the fiddle has emerged as an important part of my research, not least because I play the instrument myself. My identity as a fiddler both gives me an insider perspective ("We are both fiddlers") and highlights my different origin/status ("You're an American!"). Because of the aura of my own Americanness, I often found myself trying to convince Czech fiddlers to acknowledge the value of their music making, their re-creation of bluegrass, and the rich community life that they enjoy in the music. Perhaps the extent of "classical" violin training in the Czech Republic and its ideology of "talent" (Kingsbury 2001) makes a sense of doubt and insecurity more common among fiddlers than with other musicians.

My introduction of Franta Kacafirek, an influential fiddler from the first generation of bluegrass players whom I met toward the end of my 2007–2008 fieldwork year, provides a sense of the longer history of Czech fiddlers, but also of Czechs' challenges in approaching bluegrass fiddling. The following vignettes about younger fiddle players address the problems and possibilities they encounter in re-creating bluegrass-related music styles today. I also examine here the pragmatic motivations for Czech fiddlers' negotiation of people, sounds, and places.

BLUEGRASS AND THE FIDDLE

Since the early American colonial period and through the era of early recorded sound, fiddling has provided a forum for the negotiation of difference through music making.[2] Richard Peterson's (1997) work on the production of "authenticity" in country music emphasizes, for example, the role of older fiddlers in connecting audiences to an imagined preindustrial era and providing "representations of the unchanged past" (57) that soothed anxieties about the present.

The play of old and new that thrives in fiddle performance has made the fiddle a platform for innovative creative expression, but also a battleground for the creation and maintenance of "tradition." The fiddle sounds that have bloomed from this ground have been a key part of bluegrass music's paradoxical effectiveness as a modern and an antimodern expression.[3] Over his long career, Bill Monroe used the fiddle in his band both to shape an innovative musical style and to establish a practice of traditionalism—fiddlers can play old-time hoedowns to suggest the "down home" and can also add sophisticated musical elements (such as multipart harmony arrangements) that gesture uptown.

When Czechs encountered bluegrass music recordings via US American Forces Network broadcasts and other sources after the Second World War, they heard the variety of bluegrass fiddle styles, but not the historical context of US string band music, such as the variety of "old-time" and popular techniques and repertories familiar to US fiddlers. Without a firm technical or stylistic model, Czech bluegrass fiddlers have drawn from classical, jazz, and local folklore in their efforts to present appropriate fiddle performances.

An examination of Petr Bryndač's fiddling with the group Zelenáči reveals the eclectic stylings of Czech fiddlers during the period of their first exposure to bluegrass in the 1950s and 1960s. As shown in a Czech television clip of the band, probably from the late 1960s, Bryndač's fiddling reflects the exuberance of early Czech bluegrassers.[4] In this song, a retexting of the country classic "Before I Met You," he follows the rhythmic feel created by the band, putting a strong emphasis on the downbeat of the 3/4-time metric grid, highlighting what my Czech colleagues have often called the "polka" feel. He also uses vibrato, double-stop combinations, and emphatic triplet ornaments that sound out of place, especially when compared to recordings such as the 1954 version by Flatt and Scruggs, featuring fiddler Paul Warren.

If Bryndač's playing doesn't definitively situate his group in terms of genre, banjoist Marko Čermák's playing does. The specific technique of three-finger banjo picking is central to the signature sound of bluegrass, and thus the banjo found greater stability in the Greenhorns. While Bryndač enjoyed popularity with the band, his influence quickly faded, whereas Čermák's acclaim has included local and international awards.[5] Bryndač's successor with the Greenhorns, Franta Kacafirek, had a much more intimate engagement with bluegrass sounds and fiddling techniques—and a more lasting career.

Like many Czechs (both musicians and nonmusicians in the post–World War II period), Kacafirek began his musical career with instruction in classical violin—and with the added pressure of a father who was an accomplished flutist. After an adolescent period of resistance during which he didn't play the instrument for years, Kacafirek began an apprenticeship with a machinist. He disliked the work intensely and quit, vowing in an inspired moment that he would make his living playing the violin.

Although he began playing with Zelenáči after their period of greatest popular acclaim during the 1970s, Kacafirek was part of their continuing success. One of the most remarkable (and influential) aspects of his work with this group in the 1980s was traveling to Germany with the group to perform at the Karl May Festspiele in Elspe, Westphalia. They were one of the house bands for the event, playing and singing in evocation of the "Old West" at the park's stylized saloon.[6]

HEARING FIDDLING: OUT OF PLACE AND AT HOME

Along with his love of "America," Americans, and American music, Kacafirek expressed a brutally honest self-assessment about his ability to "play American." While he has seen some of the best fiddlers in the business (Mark O'Connor, Byron Berline, and others who have toured in the Czech Republic), his main exposure to these musicians over the past four decades has been through their recordings. The very reason that Kacafirek knows so fully that he doesn't sound like Byron Berline—an influential American fiddler—is that he has listened to Berline's records for decades, over and over and over. This prioritization of media was a necessity in the pre-1989 era, and has amplified the influence of recordings on his playing.

Kacafirek described his process of learning to re-create the renditions on these recordings as "se učit do poslední noty" (to learn to the last note). I have come to think that this perspective would privilege the left hand (the fingering or "noting" hand) over the right hand (the bowing hand). Kacafirek was quick to notice my bowing when we met in person. One of the first things that he noticed about my playing was the way I moved my right hand in using the bow. As I started into the tune "Whiskey before Breakfast," I almost stopped playing as Kacafirek exclaimed, "To je to přesně vono no, to americký!" (That's exactly it, yes, that American [way]!).[7] As I had done many times before in similar circumstances (the declaration that my playing "sounds American" has been common), I asked him to specify what exactly was "American" about my playing—what was the *vono* that he perceived?

Kacafirek explained that I used more pressure on the downward strokes of my bow, typically highlighting the off-beat. While I suggested that my heavy emphases on the off-beat are the result of my having spent years playing mandolin in a bluegrass band, he sensed in the ordering of my bowing strokes something more abstract—"Americanness."[8] In Kacafirek's case, this American *vono* seems to haunt his playing and his experiences listening to recordings, hanging slightly and frustratingly out of reach.

I should make clear here as well that Kacafirek was clearly not an amateur, in any sense of the word. A highly skilled musician and an experienced bluegrass player, he was fluent in the tunes, the songs, the styles, the licks of US bluegrass-related fiddling. He blew me away with his knowledge and his fluid incorporation of various bluegrass fiddle elements. I was so impressed that I found myself arguing with him as he repeatedly insisted that he, and other Czechs, would never be able to play like the best American fiddlers do. I am embarrassed as I listen to the interview recordings and hear myself getting flustered in my attempts to convince Kacafirek that his fiddling was idiomatically appropriate, sounded very bluegrass, and was very good. He never budged. While he would grudgingly acknowledge his skill and experience (especially in things like harmonic improvisation and soloing over chord changes), he steadfastly insisted that he would never fiddle "in an American way," not even if he sat with me every day for ten years to learn the "American" things that he hears in my playing.

In considering the gap between himself and his bluegrass fiddle ideals—and between himself and me—Kacafirek embodies more than a typical bluegrass musician's modesty. He is tracing the edge of transculture, perhaps feeling the discord of hybridity. Kacafirek's discussion of his bluegrass activity shows it to be both globally informed and localized. His playing is clearly a product of Czech desires, abilities, and circumstances, even as it is part of reference to faraway places like the Blue Ridge hills of Virginia that are often sung about in bluegrass texts, and employs musical techniques perfected for centuries around the rim of the black Atlantic. After our interview, I heard him play these sounds on an invasion barge moored on the east bank of the Vltava River in Prague, now a pub (known as the Invazák) where he would jam weekly with a group of old friends. Kacafirek's protestations about "Americanness" thus seem less about musicality and more about his negotiation of difference, his navigation of the in-between situation he has created by pursuing American fiddling as a Czech.

Franta Kacafirek's practice space at his home in Prague, Czech Republic, 2008.

Kacafirek's music making is intrinsically social and historically linked, but it is also intensely personal and tied to the moment and posture of a single listener tuned to specific and significant pieces of recorded media. There are few Czechs who are as qualified as he as a connoisseur of American fiddling, few with his performance experience—and few with such an extensive record collection. The well-handled LPs on his shelves are at the same time a ubiquitous product *and* a locally bound object. There is an aspect of simultaneity: many listeners hearing the same recorded sounds in their individual environment can bring an audience together. This "togetherness" can also highlight the distance between people, however. Kacafirek's sense of the divide between his musicality and the performances on these records is the very thing that signals to him that he is not accomplishing his goal of "playing American."

A similar paradox is at work in the fiddle tunes that Kacafirek and I both share as our "home repertory." There are common tunes and uncommon tunes—as well as tunes that wear well and tunes that are worn out—but they all circulate and resonate with significant social effects. Fiddle tunes, recordings, and bluegrass at large all offer a variety of "affordances," which opens up music as a means of "doing, thinking, and feeling" for a variety of music makers in an equally diverse variety of situations (DeNora 2003, 57). While Kacafirek's sense of distance from an idealized Americanness, his methods of approaching fiddling, and the pleasures and problems he describes are grounded in his situation and era, they are almost identical to those articulated by younger players.

JIRKA KRÁLÍK AND PLAYING "IN BETWEEN"

Jirka Králík, who belongs to the younger generation of fiddlers who have succeeded Kacafirek, stopped me cold as I sat with him playing fiddle tunes in October 2007. We had gotten together at his Prague apartment to work up some double-fiddle solos for upcoming gigs with his band the Rowdy Rascals. We were warming up, and I had just played the opening phrase of "Red Haired Boy," a standard fiddle tune in bluegrass circles, when he interrupted me: "Wait! What did you just play?" I was ready for his attribution of Americanness, but was surprised to hear him start by making specifically *musical* observations about the differences between our ways of playing the tune.

Jirka explained that he places the melody of the tune in a major-mode framework, and was surprised when I used a different mode, a difference he heard in the first notes of my performance of the tune. His version is similar to the one transcribed in *The Fiddler's Fakebook* (Brody 1983) and other common bluegrass-related media. I had changed one note (C# to D), but with this small variation—and indeed it was a variation that I had developed since I first encountered this tune playing with musicians who used these media sources of "standard" tune variants—I invoked a different musical mode.

This modality, something ascribed to many "folk" idioms (Gelbart 2007), invokes a particular relationship of sound and social structures that seems to be at play in my interaction with Jirka. For a moment, my fiddling underscored my otherness for Jirka—as an American. With my expression of harmonic difference, I became subject to a constellation of sound and identity ideals that he and other Czechs reference and draw on in their bluegrass-related music projects.

THE RECORDING ANGLE

The world of sound ideals that bluegrassers (Czech and American) draw on largely resides in sound recordings. We buy, trade, enjoy, study, and bicker about these discs and sound files, imitating and rejecting them in turn. When Jirka stopped me, he was treating me like a recording: [PAUSE], then [REWIND], then [PLAY] again, a formula that is familiar to those of us who are surrounded by contemporary recording technologies.

I felt somewhat objectified in that moment, but I played along, curious to hear and understand Jirka's reaction to my playing. Years earlier, in 2003, I had made him uncomfortable in a similar way. We had been practicing double-fiddle duet breaks for a performance with his band Sunny Side, and were packing up and talking. In a discussion about old-time music, I asked him if he was familiar with an album of string band dance music by African American musicians recorded in the 1940s. Jirka excitedly replied that he was familiar with the album, and had it in his collection. He turned to a bookcase nearby to find the disc and show it to me. I then noticed all the black nylon folders sitting on the shelf above his computer monitor. As Jirka took down a folder, he showed me that it was filled with pages of compact disc holders and with hundreds of bluegrass and old-time recordings, or, more precisely, filled with burned CD copies of albums that he had bought, traded for, and borrowed over his years of interest in Americana music. As he thumbed through pages of silver (burned) CDRs in search of the album I had mentioned, he was showing off his collection both with pride at having the recording and so many more Americana albums, and also with sheepishness at the illegal nature of his hoard. He explained that recordings are expensive; Czechs often team up to buy a box set together and then share copies of the discs. The slight discomfort that Jirka and I both encountered in navigating bluegrass music and recordings shows some of the ways in which the two are not always perfectly aligned. Sometimes musical subjects resent processes of "collection," and some compilations of recordings are not entirely legally or socially sanctioned.

OTHERNESS AND ITS DISCONTENTS

In a discussion I had with Jirka Králík some time after our experience playing "Red Haired Boy," he echoed Kacafirek's sentiments about the persisting foreignness of American-style fiddling. With tacit reference to the sort of *vono* that Kacafírek articulated as an ideal, Jirka found a specific case of difference in language. He cited the difference in accent in the pronunciation of English and Czech as a reason that it is difficult for Czechs to play the fiddle in an idiomatically "American" way. Czech speakers use a strong accent on the initial syllable of each word, an effect that Jirka likened to "a sack of potatoes falling down stairs." Spoken American English, he countered, feels to him more like waves on the ocean. His conception of Czech and American language thus sets up a divide: plodding Czechness that thuds down an imaginary set of steps into a dark basement, versus Americanness as something like going to the beach—the waves he imagines could be more interestingly chaotic, producing a steady wash of pleasingly unpredictable rhythms and timbres.[9]

While Kacafirek envisions limits in approaching Americanness, Jirka sometimes seems to resent his Czechness—at least in his conception of himself as a musician. In his value judgments against his own Czech linguistic rhythms, he voices ambivalence about his own perceived ability to adapt his musicality to the American styles he loves and works so hard to emulate. Another particular area where he feels challenged in his pursuit of Americana is his refined training in music theory and performance.

When Jirka used the phrase "tone materials" in discussing my modal suggestion in "Red Haired Boy," he was ready to engage on a deep level in a discussion of music theory and its application in performance. As part of his education at the Jaroslav Ježek Conservatory in Prague, he studied scales intensely, and in our rehearsal and performances together he has analyzed musical elements quickly and in detail. But this intense attention to detail, besides being helpful, can also be experienced as a limitation. Jirka mapped his frustration onto a body-mind dichotomy, saying that his scale-oriented understandings of music are "more in here [pointing to his head] than in the hands."[10]

I asked him if by referring to "tone materials" he meant different scales, and he replied, "Not exactly scales, but you choose the different tones to be important in a scale." Following Jirka's way of thinking, then, it is the choices between the notes that would transform simple (Czech) playing into compelling American-style fiddling. Jirka is frustrated by the difficulty in emulating not the notes, but the sensibilities that lie between the notes. Here, "being bluegrass" takes on a specific import as the basis for musicality. I articulated my thoughts about music and identity to Jirka by asking him how he thinks that Czechs deal with musical "style," and how "who you are affects how you play." He responded, "What we're trying is not to change, but to pretend a different heritage and different identity. And we play music which doesn't belong, which has nothing to do with our identity."[11] It is ironic that Jirka feels limited by his technical knowledge; his musical vocabulary is extensive but does not always seem applicable in the musical conversation that he wishes to have, the bluegrass that he wishes to play.

Over the years that I have known him, Jirka has adapted both in his musicality and in his sense of vocation. We first worked on twin fiddling to perform with his band in 2002–2003, Sunny Side, traditionalists who wore cowboy hats and old-timey string ties. His playing from that time was similarly traditionalist, following the pattern of Byron Berline, Kenny Baker, and other tune-oriented fiddlers. He succeeded in the bluegrass realm, winning the "Best Fiddler" award from the Bluegrass Association of the Czech Republic two times, in 1998 and 2002.

The author and Jirka Králík playing fiddles with Sunny Side at Klub Cl-5 in the Smíchov suburb of Prague, Czech Republic, 2003.

Jirka's group the Rowdy Rascals first focused on old-time material from the 1920s and '30s. After Jirka completed a course in instrument making and began his jazz studies at the Ježek Conservatory in 2004, he continued his contacts with musicians in the United States, finding inspiration in groups like the Hot Club of Cowtown, who play more jazzy material. Later he billed the Rascals as a "Western Swing Band," and retained respect in the European bluegrass community, with invited performances at the Norwegian Risør Bluegrass Festival and workshop and the European World of Bluegrass festival in La Roche-sur-Foron, France. In 2010 I helped Jirka connect with an American clogging group; he was later hired as their bandleader and fiddler for tours in the Czech Republic, Poland, and Turkey.

Early on, Jirka seemed determined to make music his livelihood, but unlike Franta, he was not able to find venues for work. He now is part of the family engineering firm, and while he still plays as a hobby, as of 2016 he says that he has found other interests. In addition to his personal and career concerns, however, Jirka's concerns seem part of his move away from bluegrass. I will next discuss the experiences of another fiddler who pursues music as an avocation. Unlike Jirka, she has found ways to incorporate polished technique into bluegrass-related musicality.

SLÁVKA FRANCLÍKOVÁ AND "CATCHING" BLUEGRASS

I met Slávka Franclíková in 2008 at the bluegrass workshop organized by the Petr Brandejs Band, where I was a participant observer in the fiddle class, and Jirka Králík was teaching. Like Jirka and many Czech fiddlers I have worked with, Slávka first encountered the violin at a music school. She took violin lessons in her hometown, the North Bohemian city of Liberec, one the largest municipalities in the region after Prague and Pilsen, located near the northern border with Germany and Poland. Like most middle-class Czechs that I know, while Slávka was studying (art and design at a specialized vocational school) in Prague, she maintained close ties to her hometown. One of the major activities that brought her back to Liberec was music, in particular her band Namodro.

During a visit home in 2004, Slávka performed what she called *klasika* or *vážná hudba* (classical, serious music) with some fellow students at an art opening in a nearby town. After the event, she and another of the violinists went to a party in Liberec where the bluegrass band Namodro was playing. The members of the group were actively searching for a fiddler, and asked the two violinists if they were interested in trying to play bluegrass. Slávka found her way fairly well because some of what the group played sounded familiar from her childhood experiences hearing Czech folk and country music at home:

> My mom with my dad played some . . .
> on guitars
> so I heard there a few songs that I knew.[12]

Her parents are part of the generation who experienced the first wave of interest in country as a mainstream pop phenomenon in the 1970s. Slávka later explained that she had never listened to country music as her parents did, and still prefers classical and pop music. Still, her parents' listening (and playing) practices had provided her with a framework that the other musician didn't have during that first encounter with Namodro. Bluegrass is often considered (jokingly) to be contagious, and it is—for the right person—easily "caught." For Slávka, the fit between music repertory and her own competency worked; she "caught" it,

> and that second violinist
> she didn't catch it
> because she didn't know [the music] at all and
> the next day they had already called me
> [to say] that I caught it pretty well
> that it worked with me
> and if I would like to play with them
> if I would like to try it . . .
> and from that time all I listen to
> or mostly all I listen to is bluegrass . . .
> and from the beginning they thought
> that I joined the band just so I could try it
> that bluegrass doesn't really do it for me
> yeah
> they thought
> that
> that I am young, and listen to techno
> which isn't true
> and it came out after two years when I kept on with them
> you know
> how I really like this bluegrass
> which is true.[13]

To use the sort of evangelistic vocabulary that bluegrassers across the globe use to speak about conversions to bluegrass, I could also say that the music caught her. To the surprise of the older, male members of Namodro, bluegrass has held Slávka's interest consistently for a number of years, and she performed with the group until moving to New Zealand in 2013.[14] My discussion with her about how she learned to play after her "conversion experience" brought out the fact that "catching" bluegrass is not always easy, and usually involves hard work.

FIDDLE INSPIRATIONS AND ASPIRATIONS

Slávka has set herself an ambitious set of inspirations. She named Stéphane Grappelli, Mark O'Connor, and Vassar Clements as her major influences and models. The polish, complexity, and artistry she sensed in recordings by these musicians made her excited to be playing the fiddle. Namodro has proved to be a fit for her in terms of style, as they are working on musical projects that fit the musical ideals that Slávka holds. In an aside during our formal interview, she talked about how early on she discovered her preference for the more polished style that she now pursues:

> when
> someone starts to play bluegrass
> then they realize how many bands here
> just play into the air . . .
> like they
> make three chords on the guitar
> you know
> and pass that off as music
> and it is music in its own way
> but I don't appreciate it . . .
> I appreciate bluegrass
> just
> bluegrass and classical.[15]

In both classical music and the sort of bluegrass projects that Slávka prefers, she indicates a preference for sophisticated tunes and arrangements, for what she called later in our interview "quality" music. Quality music has sophisticated musical arrangements and virtuosity that for her are based in technical mastery of the fiddle. Slávka is a polished player, but she is frustrated by her inability to play things that she hears, especially the breakdown-style playing of the early generations of bluegrass fiddlers, such as Vassar Clements, Chubby Wise, and Bobby Hicks. Due to her classical training and her own particular taste as someone who enjoys listening to fiddling, Slávka is more attracted to (and more able to play) fiddle styles that emphasize nuanced phrasing and longer, carefully joined melodic lines than to those that are more riff-based and emphasize "hot" chord-based improvisation.

Likewise, Slávka spoke about how Namodro has certain musical desires that they are not always able to fulfill. The "newgrass" style that some other members of the band prefer to listen to and would like to perform is technically difficult, and to be effective in performance, it must be "on":

> you have to really know it
> and when it's played just willy nilly
> like, that just isn't it [*vono*].[16]

She then described how the group eventually decided that they would not strive to be something they are not:

> . . . we just decided that we will do it for
> fun
> and we have to respect that,
> that not everyone is willing
> to dedicate themselves to it
> or they are willing but don't have time
> they have to take care of family
> so we decided
> that we will just let it flow
> we won't push somewhere needlessly
> travel around
> and promote ourselves.[17]

From making a distinction in terms of genre and technique, Slávka quickly moved into discussion of a wider realm. It is not simply a musical problem that keeps Namodro from progressing in their musicality. Families, jobs, and other time and energy commitments don't allow the members of the band to realize their ambition to play newgrass-type music, and perhaps to make the band a larger part of their lives. Slávka also explained that some members of Namodro play with other bands (one of them plays in at least three) to express different aspects of their musicality, be it rock, blues, or newgrass. With Namodro, though, they perform bluegrass in ways that create a compromise between the members' aesthetic and practical concerns. In the words of their self-description on their website, "The group plays modern bluegrass and newgrass repertory, mainly taken from American stars of that genre, exclusively with our own Czech texts, but on request we can dip into the golden pool of Czech country or tramp music."[18] Namodro's repertory is a mix that doesn't extend too far into the realm of progressive bluegrass: the most "newgrassy" number documented in videos on their website is "Nashville Skyline Rag." The group shines on bluegrass standards such as "Rocky Top" and "Love, Please Come Home," which are featured along with a Czech-language version of "Great Balls of Fire" and other US songs with new Czech texts.

As Slávka put it, these musicians just play for fun. In a typical Czech turn, this involves frequent trips to the pub. She concluded her discussion of Namodro's negotiation of time, genre, and relationships by explaining that

> every week we go to U Kozy
> it's just a pub
> like a cabin in the middle of the woods
> there it's very
> very natural
> there's a fireplace and
> mostly tramps go there
> yeah but we go there
> almost every week
> and basically it's enough for fun.[19]

"DOWNLOADING" MUSIC (MANUALLY) IN THE DIGITAL AGE

In our interview in February 2008, Slávka described her process of learning fiddle tunes and technique using the Czech verb *stáhnout*. This word can mean a number of seemingly contradictory things: to pull or peel off (as in skinning an animal), to pull, tighten, or roll on (as with a hat or belt or sock), or to withdraw (as from a bank) (Fronek 1999, 1103–1104). In my Czech experiences, however, I have heard *stáhnout* (or the verb's imperfective equivalent, *stahovat*) most often used in a variation on that last definition—as the verb for transferring (or perhaps "pulling out") information from the internet.[20] In today's web-oriented culture, *stáhnout* is the equivalent term for "download."

I was surprised to hear Slávka use this word-concept in this way—not least because of my imagining of what the process of downloading music into a musician's body would entail. In interactions with fiddlers after this interview, I would ask how they learned tunes and other material, and inevitably the word *stáhnout* would arise in their descriptions. In my interview protocol, I eventually came to ask the question using the vocabulary that Slávka and others had taught me. When I asked Kacafirek how he had learned his version of the Texas-style fiddle tune "Cattle in the Cane," I used the verb: "Jak jsi to stahnul?" (How did you transcribe/download/learn it?) The tricky part about this word, as Slávka and Kacafirek both explained, was that it refers to transcription, but can also mean much more. I asked for a clarification the first time Slávka used it, employing a Czech cognate of "transcribe," *transkribovat*. She assented when I compared the word to the process of "to hear and then write," but she specified her exact method, which uses a certain piece of computer software named, fittingly enough, Transcriber:

> it's a program that slows down the solo for you
> without changing the key
> and this Víťa [an older bandmate]
> he told me about when
> in communism nothing was here
> any bluegrass recording that was possible to get
> was on reel-to-reel tape
> so he slowed it by half, but he had to completely retune
> like an octave lower
> the banjo, yeah
> but thanks to that Transcriber, nothing like that [is required now].[21]

The historical precedent that Slávka provides for her own learning process grounds her approach in a long-standing Czech tradition of learning through recordings. But the ways in which she uses technology (including now nearly ubiquitous globalized information networks) and the ways she talks about them give a new resonance to the act of extracting musical elements from sound recordings. The motions of learning undertaken by Slávka and other Czech bluegrassers in their performance and pedagogy projects result in the sedimentation of a collective memory of bluegrass, an active, generative knowing of this music (Connerton 1989).

Despite their desire for fidelity in emulation and their significant efforts, the version of bluegrass that Czechs are rooted in is not the same soil as bluegrass music's home turf. The sedimented knowledge of bluegrass that Czechs have worked so hard to download, understand, and use is very different from the layers of knowing and doing—of *being*—bluegrass in the United States. In Czech bluegrass discourse, there are understandings that are unintelligible or even irrelevant to American bluegrassers.

I have characterized Slávka as a classically oriented musician who is uncomfortable with some aspects of American fiddling, and she is—by her own admission—often shy on stage. However, I also must describe her as highly proficient in being part of a musical happening such as the weekly jam at the Prague pub U Supa, where I often saw her and played with her, Jirka Králík, and other local musicians. She was always ready to try to play a

Fiddler Slávka Franclíková at a weekly bluegrass jam, U Supa, Prague, Czech Republic, 2008.

break, even if she faltered or "fell off" the melody halfway through. Although she has struggled with some musical aspects, she became a full member of the band Namodro because she clearly loves the music, and is working to integrate herself into the modes of understanding that other jammers share.

The Czech language distinguishes varieties of "knowing" with the separate words *znát* (knowing of, knowing how) and *vědět* (knowing that). Slávka distinguished two different sorts of work-knowing in her musicality: practice as in "practicing an instrument," and practice as in the praxis of making music in a social setting:

> When I play at jams
> so that's my instruction
> and when I'm home I have
> absolutely
> no plan as I should have
> like if I were to sit and play scales.[22]

The "knowing that" aspects of music, technical proficiency in scales and other music theory–based exercises, while necessary to musical participation, are often subsidiary to the "knowing how" of social interaction. Slávka's description of bluegrass jams as the site of her learning indicates that while the isolated experience of instrumental practice is important, the most important part of the work and play involved with the music is the understanding and personal interaction of "being bluegrass."

EXPRESSION AND PLAYING "FROM WITHIN"

Slávka, while comfortable in the social scene of the music, still strives to learn and understand the music in new and deeper ways. Her frustrations in this process are many. The relationship between ability and ideals—what one would like to play and what one *can* play (or what one feels comfortable playing for others) involves self-searching and a great deal of negotiation between work and play. The extent to which Slávka works on her music makes me almost reluctant to call it "play."

After speaking with Slávka about some of the parts of fiddling that she finds difficult, I asked her what she finds easy about playing the fiddle, a question that sparked further conversation about what she finds most pleasurable to play:

> generally I like
> slower songs
> since
> because they don't stress me out
> and I have a chance to compose [*vytvořit*] something nice.

Besides "compose," other meanings of *vytvořit* include acts of framing as well as more straightforward creation. When I followed up on her suggestion about her creative input in her playing, asking if she had some sort of personal playing style, however, Slávka said no.

> LB: Not at all?
> SF: I think not
> I'm capable of playing something according to someone
> that I know
> LB: like according to what they played
> SF: yeah
> but basically
> I would have to improvise
> to have my own style
> you know
> and improvising
> so that it is nice
> I don't know how
> so that doesn't concern me now

> but if I will keep improving, year by year
> until I am sixty, then maybe I will
> maybe I will have my own style.[23]

I agree with Slávka's self-assessment, and followed up on these points when I gave her a lesson in return for her time in our interview. The steadiness of her bowing and the sweetness of her tone are strong points I notice in her playing. Slávka's violin training has given her a solid technique, so she feels comfortable with the subtle control of timbre and volume that gives pleasing shape to slower pieces that express wistfulness or serenity instead of boisterous energy. She is less able to use the expressive registers of pitch and timbre variation and rhythmic syncopation as well as the repertory of riffs that lend compelling shape and character to the harmonic-improvisation-based "breakdown" mode of fiddling.

Richard Peterson (1997, 138) has identified two aspects of US country music practices, the "parlor" and the "frolic." This distinction differentiates polished, intimate forms (ballads, sentimental songs, and contemplative instrumental music) from the rowdier, more rustic, dance-oriented and masculine-associated forms (outdoor music, dance music, group singing) (Malone 2002, 20–21).[24] Slávka is not alone in her tendency toward the parlor—I have observed that many Czech bluegrassers tend to stick to the notes they have studiously learned from recordings. This situation is similar to that of many American players beginning with the music. I would argue that to some degree, Czechs seem less likely than many of their American counterparts to explore unknown rhythmic or tonal territories in their playing and singing, sticking more closely to set melodies.

Gender expectations are a factor here (the parlor is often considered a feminine space), but not the only one. I find that Slávka's experience is not entirely a result of gendered roles in the Czech Republic, but might be a factor that emerges from the musical and larger cultural practices in the country, perhaps due to the thriving tradition of music education in schools, the culture of "rule following," or more subtle elements of cultural life.

DAVID KOUCKÝ AND ANOTHER WAY OF FIDDLING

Another young musician, David Koucký, has quickly become one of the top fiddlers in the Czech bluegrass scene. A skilled bassist who also plays bluegrass and old-time banjo styles, he eventually decided to learn fiddle as well. He has played with a number of Czech groups, including the well-established bluegrass band BG Cwrkot. David's rise to Czech bluegrass prominence is notable not only for its swiftness; his fiddling is rough-edged, rowdy, and much more in the "frolic" tradition than the polished sounds created and appreciated by Slávka and Jirka.

I first heard of David from Slávka, who mentioned his help as an important contribution to her early development as a fiddler. Her account of the experience indicates some of the tendencies of Czechs as they encounter new music and work to incorporate it into their own musicality. Slávka met David at U Kozy, the pub in North Bohemia where her band plays on a regular basis. Despite their different styles of fiddling—or perhaps because of them—she learned a great deal from David, not just about a certain song, but about how to play the fiddle as a fiddle and not a violin.

> when I met him
> he had played the fiddle for half a year
> of course in technique
> it was bad
> but when he played something
> well, there it was.

In Slávka's perception, David had that certain something, the "it" or *vono* that she felt she lacked. That evening, she asked him to help her with a tune she was working on. She had worked to transcribe and learn (*stáhnout*) the piece but was missing something that she found with David's help:

> he taught me "Foggy mountain breakdown"
> he just showed me
> and "of course"
> I had learned it
> I had it down
> I had transcribed it
> I sort of had it down
> I had learned it somewhat
> but here something was missing
> I had learned it some
> but here it was weird somehow
> and he then
> he played it for me
> and everything was connected
> and he just helped me
> with how it goes
> how it is.

When I asked her to clarify, Slávka played the section that she was "missing" in her own learning process, a descending cadential phrase that closed out the main melody of this famous Earl Scruggs banjo tune.

> I knew that there was something
> but I didn't know how the fingers ran and such
> and he sort of
> said,
> "See, it's terribly simple."[25]

David could make the movement that eluded Slávka in her pursuit of a credible version of "Foggy Mountain Breakdown." In showing her how to end the phrase, he closed a part of the gap that she felt between where she was and where she would like to be. Whether Slávka's more parlor-oriented way of playing represents some sort of lack in her technique or musicianship (something that will be corrected or augmented with time, as she opines) or if this is simply an expression of her style as a fiddler remains an open question.

A BLOOD RELATION

I don't know where David procured the know-how about the descending melodic figure. He might have seen or heard a recording (a YouTube clip, perhaps) that highlighted that melodic segment more clearly, or he may have experienced it in a live performance or jam. He might even have found the tune in the form of written notation that spelled out the melody—but he knew and could play it in a way that was *vono* for Slávka.

The bassist and bandleader of BG Cwrkot, Pavel "Brandy" Brandejs, points to another possible source for David's intuitive grasp of how to play the fiddle. Brandy joked about Koucký's short learning curve by way of introducing him at a concert at which the group performed in October 2007:

> The youngest person playing with me is
> a man from Mlada Boleslav
> he's playing with me now for a year
> for those who are here studying fiddle
> I'd like to startle you with knowing that
> with me he's been playing fiddle a year, and has only been playing fiddle
> at all for a year and a half
> [laughing]
> he's got it in his blood
> from Mlada Boleslav
> David Koucký.[26]

Perhaps it is a throwaway remark, a remark that could be made about anyone with such a story. But with David, the situation is exceptional—in a way that is awkward, at least for me. For years as part of the Czech bluegrass scene, I had heard of a fiddle player in the Czech Republic who was—to use one of the more polite derogatory phrases commonly used in Czech—a *cikán*, a member of the marginalized Roma ethnic group. Through further conversations with Czech bluegrassers (including with Slávka, who is a friend of David and who gave me his email address), I learned that David was this person.

Zuzana Jurková's (2007, 114) work on Roma music and with Roma musicians considers the Roma worthy of academic and ethnographic study, which is still a somewhat rare opinion.[27] The gap between Roma and "white" Czechs, as the common term denotes the difference, is widespread in Czech history, with many instances of systematic educational, financial, and social marginalization. Manifestations of anti-Roma sentiment and activism in the Czech Republic include a wall erected in the late 1990s through the North Bohemian town of Ústí nad Labem to separate a so-called "Czech" neighborhood from an (implicitly non-Czech) Roma housing area (Barany 2002, 191–200).

After working with Jurková and other Czech scholars, I have become more aware of the many problems that Roma (both musicians and the general population) encounter within Czech society, even as Roma music is often celebrated. Therefore, while I am impressed with David's musicianship and his charisma in front of the microphone, I am wary of joining in on what seems to be a general consensus among my friends in the Czech bluegrass scene who talk about David as a different sort of person. Most of them imply, while not saying outright, that his ethnicity, family, and community background mark him as unusual in some way.

I have often been introduced by Czechs using my name with an added epithet: Lee z Ameriky (Lee from America). This phrase is a reminder to me that I can be reified and essentialized as a figure of "Americanness" in the same way that David is encompassed by the discourses of ethnicity in Central Europe. I'm usually marked only by my voice; while sometimes I can pass linguistically, either my stumbling Czech or my practiced English usually gives me away. Unlike David, though, I can slip into a crowd and not be visibly different from the rest of the white folks.

My Americanness might have presented a barrier in this case. While I had met and spoken with David several times over the years, he had been reluctant to speak with me and record an interview, saying that he was not good enough to rate inclusion in my work. When I was finally able to interview him in May 2016, David told touching stories of how music became a place of refuge for him during a difficult childhood—and surprised me by saying

David Koucký with fiddle and homemade Confederate military hat, at his home in the countryside north of Prague, Czech Republic, 2016.

that he had constructed his own version of a Confederate military cap, and had recently ordered a Confederate flag.

In contrast to Pavel Brandejs's hint of a biological connection, David's interest in bluegrass seems more about affinity—especially the fact that costuming affords him a way to take on another identity and join others with a similar interest. Visiting David's home, I saw instrument cases and signs of Americanist hobbyism all around. However, I also saw that he had constructed an entire costume for a mid-eighteenth-century Scottish Highlander, including a homemade and functional muzzle-loading musket!

Czech bluegrassers create imaginative links to Americanness, but reinforce their own Czechness as they perform "America" (or other place/time

Audience member wearing a rebel flag shirt at the Banjo Jamboree festival, 2003.

imaginaries). In the United States and elsewhere, whiteness and country music are often united under a Confederate flag, and African Americans have a marginal place in Appalachia, and in bluegrass music.[28] The ethnic divisions in the Czech Republic are deep, with nationalist, fascist, and white power groups a vocal part of political life. It seems possible that these Czech "rebels" might, in their own affinities, link southern US racism with their Czech nationalism. This concern is a topic for further study. I remain hopeful that bluegrass might serve as a way for Czechs of differing social classes, ethnicities, and socioaesthetic backgrounds to imagine and create some kind of common ground, as has sometimes been the case with American bluegrass.[29]

My photo of David Koucký shows him taking on an attitude and clothing that seem antiquated. After I took the photo, I showed it to him, and he commented, excitedly, that it looked "old-time," and asked if I would email him a copy. David has also started playing an open-backed banjo, a standard element in what US players call an "old-time string band." This relatively recent area of Czech Americanism affords new ways for Czechs to imagine their connections to the United States, and to Americanness.

CZECH OLD-TIME

My right-hand technique is a constant source of comments from Czech bluegrassers, especially fiddlers who are experienced enough to notice the "feel" that I play with. More than once, a Czech fiddler has called the way I play an "old-timeový shuffle," suggesting not chronological distance, but a distinction of style—old-time, not bluegrass. Since I began fieldwork in the Czech Republic, I have become more interested in repertories and styles known as "old-time," dance and vocal music based in pre-bluegrass commercial recordings, later field recordings, and folk-revivalist re-creations. I have been so taken with recordings of the Foghorn Stringband, Bruce Molsky, and others that at times I have played this style and material more than bluegrass—especially during my graduate school years in Charlottesville, Virginia, where I joined a vibrant old-time music scene.

As a fieldworker, a foreigner, and a cultural outsider in the Czech Republic, I have also used this style description as a way to cover up my own insecurity as a performer and deal with my intimidation by the skilled Czech players I have encountered and played with. I have often described myself as an "old-time fiddler" to Czechs who are aware of this alternate string band style, sometimes as a way of apologizing for my rusty bluegrass chops. Since "old-time" was a lesser-known term and style, using it could be a way to place myself outside the Czech bluegrass world, as it might minimize my aura as a bluegrass fiddler authenticated by my American origins.

I have followed with great interest as old-time string band music has become more popular in the Czech Republic. Czech old-time music performer and publicizer Martin Žák has been of great practical help to his fellow Czechs who are interested in learning this way of making music. Over the last decades, Žák has published and performed extensively; his website indicates the extent of his activities:

> Since 1992 Martin Žák has been taking care of his specialised store with musical instruments and sheet music and has gathered much precious experience

> in this field. He has also published a series of books on music and also written some of them. His most memorable book so far is called "Banjo dávných horalů, farmářů, kovbojů, tuláků a jiných dobrodruhů" (Banjo of Old Mountaineers, Farmers, Cowboys, Hobos and Other Adventurers) (Country Home 2002). This book (accompanied with a CD) includes, among many other things, Martin's own findings from his trip through [the] U.S. South-East where he went in 1999 to search for the roots of his beloved music.[30]

Žák began his Americanist efforts within the bluegrass and tramping circles, and then became more familiar with and then fascinated with US old-time string band music. His passion for this subgenre has almost singlehandedly brought its trademark techniques and sounds to Czech musicians.

One of the signature sounds of the old-time string band is a banjo played not with the three-finger Scruggs "roll," which uses finger picks to strike the strings from below, but with a down-stroke clawhammer style that strikes them from above. These playing methods produce different melodic and chordal configurations than do bluegrass-style banjo techniques, and are one of the most common characteristics used to differentiate the two string band approaches.[31] Žák plays and teaches (in person, in recordings, and

*Czech old-time musician Martin Žák (**second row, second from right**) and students at his Old-Time Music Workshop in the South Bohemian countryside, Czech Republic, 2009.*

in books) old-time banjo styles, most often referred to simply as "clawhammer."

Over the last ten years of participant observation, I have been curious about the spread of old-time music in the Czech Republic, since old-time string bands are in the main dominated by the fiddle sound, and are led, in most cases, by a fiddler. How could this style be taken up at the same time that Czechs involved in bluegrass-related music making complain that there are not enough fiddle players and their playing is not up to snuff?

GROUNDING THE MUSIC WITH RAKOVNICKEJ POTOK

In August 2009, I met with the members of a band from Rakovník, a small town about fifty kilometers northwest of Prague. Rakovnickej Potok (Rakovník Creek) are a four-piece band that specializes in performance of bluegrass and old-time US string band repertory and style. I had been eager to meet this group since seeing them in a YouTube video in 2006. I was particularly interested in their fiddler, Jan "Honza" Čermák (no relation to Marko), who, in videos I saw online, employed a fair amount of syncopation, breaking the "polka" emphasis on the downbeat and other main pulse points.

In interviews, I generally ask fiddlers—and other musicians—to describe difficulties they have had in learning to play the fiddle in the context of US string band music—as well as the parts of their efforts that they feel are satisfying and successful. While I try to keep the conversation focused on musicality and the experience of performance, these discussions inevitably become personal, most often focusing on differences between our own playing styles.

My interview with Rakovnickej Potok took place outside the workshop where their banjo player at the time, Jindřich "Jindra" Matuška, builds open-backed banjos in his spare time. It was a beautiful day, and we enjoyed getting to know each other. After I introduced my project and posed my standard interview questions to the band, they wanted to play some tunes. I was glad to share a musical moment with them, but knew that the typical problems would probably ensue. I would be cast as their exotic other, and the typical lines of "difference" would emerge. Honza commented after we had played a few tunes:

> this style of playing that you play is richer than mine
> [mine] is sort of flat [square]
> simpler
> much simpler.[32]

Jan "Honza" Čermák (fiddler) and Petr Hejkal (banjoist) of Rakovnickej Potok, at our interview in Rakovník, Czech Republic, 2009.

When we talked afterward, Honza and the other band members proposed their theories to explain the difference in our playing styles: that I live a few hours' drive from the birthplace of many important US string band musicians, or that I have been immersed in the linguistic rhythms of southern US English. I protested that I also grew up playing Suzuki method classical violin and only started saying "y'all" halfway through my undergrad years at the University of North Carolina.

I would argue that there is a more specifically musical reason for the playing difference. Recently I have been experimenting with the rhythmically complex right-hand technique that Bruce Molsky has spread in the contemporary old-time scene, as well as the microtonal variations audible in recordings of early twentieth-century US fiddlers. Honza's way of playing—a more restrained or, as he put it, "clean" style—has plenty of US exponents, but I had a hard time convincing him of the stylistic appropriateness of his playing. Honza maintained that he did not know how to add to his playing the ornaments or accents that would *zautentizovat* his playing—make it sound authentically American in some way. He continued by saying that pitch flexibility was his biggest challenge:

> I have an excellent ear
> I practically can't play out of tune
> It just doesn't work
> it goes against my heart
> I want to play cleanly.[33]

Honza articulates more clearly the sort of tension that Slávka Franclíková suggested in her description of what is difficult for her to play. His desire to play a certain way is thwarted by some sort of limitation—intriguingly, though, the limit here is something deep within himself. Honza is attracted to the old-time style, even though its rougher aspects don't fit with what he feels is his innate musical sensibility, his "heart." His use of biological terms finds historical precedent in postsocialist Europe. The relationship between an essential core and the "authenticating" ornamentation of a fiddle tune follows the double-consciousness model often used to describe the coping mechanisms of citizens negotiating self-realization during state socialism.

The idea of a "double consciousness" is, of course, rooted in discourse about African American identity politics, which, through the performance and representation of "blackness" in American music, also informs my understanding of Czech fiddling. While the legacy of racially marked popular culture is not clearly visible in most Czech bluegrass,[34] traces of the politics of representation involved can emerge through Czech Americanism in unexpected ways.

Barry Shank has written eloquently about the creation of a performing self by which musicians evoke ideals that they wish to convey through performance. While Shank's case studies are typically grounded in specific issues such as black-white racial dynamics and folk versus popular debates, they suggest ways to consider the performance of Americana musics in non-US contexts. I suspect that in their "heart" many Czech musicians sense what Shank (2002, 110–111) calls an "imaginary perceptible difference" as they demarcate the boundary between themselves and their musical ideal, US string band sounds. Shank sees Bob Dylan expressing this sense of difference through gravel-voiced singing and the constricted gasp of the harmonica; Kacafirek sensed a possibility for it in my right-hand emphases, and Jirka Králík in my use of a modal sound.

The sense of difference these gestures afford Czechs is significant: I suspect that even after 1989's opening to the West, mediated images of the United States are less powerful than they were for musicians like Franta Kacafirek. Bluegrass retains its power as an escape from daily life as an alternative socio-aesthetic world because many Czechs still imagine and embody it as "foreign."

In Ladislav Holý's (1996, 65) anthropological investigation of "Czechness," he found that many Czechs believe that to be truly "Czech" you have to not only live in the Czech lands and speak Czech, but also have "Czech" parents and be socialized in a normative "Czech" way. By extension, therefore, they feel that it is as difficult for them to present themselves in an "American" way as it is for someone else to perform "Czechness."

This strict notion of identity applies only to "lower-other" participants in Czech sociopolitics, it seems. While Roma heritage, for example, is an obstacle to participation in Czech society, Czech heritage does not exclude the possibility of performing "Americanness," if not taking on an "Americanish" identity whole hog. Czechs persist in playing bluegrass and other US string band styles, resolving in various ways the distance they feel between themselves and the music to which they are devoted. I personally resolve this gap by considering how Czechs have actually moved across the boundary between "Czech" and "American," establishing transcultural (re)creations of American music in what I call the interstitial or liminal "play space" of Czech bluegrass. Although perhaps not all the way "across" the divide between "Czech" and "American," these folks have placed themselves somewhere, significantly, "in between."

THE "HEART" AND CREATIVITY

With all the mentions of the circulatory system, biological difference, and other bodily concepts by my Czech fiddler colleagues, I bring us back to the "heart" of identity. The "heart" not only can lead to exclusive stances on nationality or musical identity, it can be the site of creative innovation, where the experience of music is deep enough to feel as natural as a heartbeat. Jirka Králík self-diagnosed a gap between the head and hands; Slávka Franclíková described her difficulties finding something to play "from within herself" in a bluegrass style. Honza of Rakovnickej Potok, in addition to saying how his "heart" seemed to limit his musicality in fiddling, also linked "heart" to creativity:

> I play with my heart [*srdcem*]
> I don't study the theory of this music . . .
> We are Czechs
> we don't try to imitate foreign music,
> but we make music that we like,
> which is close to our heart.
> We do it our own way
> that means that even this style is our own.[35]

This paradox of the heart seems all too familiar—it is both a limitation and a source of liberation. Ironically, it is because Honza is an outsider himself that he can engage with his heart. He is not as avid a fan or a researcher of bluegrass or old-time as the other members of Rakovnickej Potok. He can commit to playing the music, enjoying the music, being the music, without the frictions of critical discourse, of intellectualization, of other problematizations related to "knowing that"—he knows "how" to play.

For the other members of Rakovnickej Potok I spoke with, old-time might be a way to live out their bluegrass-related desires in a way that Honza does within their group—without pressure, cares, or friction. Banjoist Jindra spoke of their switch from playing bluegrass to old-time as a way of more fully realizing their goals for playing music. Their interpretation of the old-time style emphasizes its homophonic texture and less virtuosic instrumental playing. Bluegrass, as they explained revealingly, usually features individual instrumental solos, often in an atmosphere of competition and contestation. If we believe what they are saying, then we must consider what they do not as an *imitation* (with varying degrees of success or failure), but as a renegotiation of what American string band music has become sonically, experientially, and semantically in the Czech context.

At the end of my visit, I wanted to tell the members of Rakovnickej Potok that their music making really did ground this music in a new way, and had created a new community that seemed to flourish in its place. "Líbí se mi jak se spojujete" (I like how you connect with each other), I said. In reply, Jindra, the banjo player and cofounder of the group, reversed this relation of the musicians, the music, and the process of connecting: "Vona ta muzika spojuje" (It's the music that connects us).[36]

5

SINGING TRUTH, FIDELITY, AND PLAY IN CZECH BLUEGRASS GOSPEL

PERFORMING GOSPEL: RELIÉF ON STAGE

On the evening of November 13, 2007, the members of Reliéf were nearing the end of their second set of songs at the downtown Prague club Balbínova Poetická Hospůdka, or as it is nicknamed, the Balbínka.[1] The group had so far displayed virtuosity through trading instrumental breaks on mandolin, guitar, banjo, and resophonic slide guitar over the steady beat of the bass. All four members supported the vocal sound, belting out songs with the signature up-tempo "drive" of bluegrass and crooning others to a more languid country-ballad lope (and on a few occasions, setting their instruments down to perform *a cappella* gospel songs, which are highly prized by their audiences).

I was in the audience, a few months into a year-long fieldwork stay in the Czech Republic, and was glad to be in contact with Reliéf, one of the most highly regarded groups in the vibrant Czech bluegrass scene. Especially curious about Reliéf's interpretations of gospel songs, I hoped, through follow-up interviews with the band members, to learn more about the group's negotiations in performing sacred material.

As a relatively young group (the members were born in the late 1970s and early 1980s), Reliéf inherited existing traditions of grafting Czech modes of creating meaning onto adopted American music, as well as the resulting expressive performative spaces and social possibilities that "Czech" bluegrass affords. Reliéf's negotiation of gospel material brings up issues of personal

Reliéf performing at the Balbínova Poetická Hospůdka, Prague, Czech Republic, 2007.

belief, aesthetic preferences, and stylistic fidelity. Here I highlight the bodily and socioaesthetic dispositions as well as the musical sounds and performative contextualization in which the band's members resolve their internal differences and create compelling and truthful performances of gospel material.

Toward the end of the second and final set that evening in 2007, guitarist and interlocutor Jirka Holoubek shuffled around in conference with the rest of the band and then stepped up to the microphone to introduce the next piece, carrying out his job as emcee through banter with the Czech audience:

> The next-to-last song will be *a cappella*
> we didn't think originally that we'd include it
> because in recent years
> we've sung it a lot
> but we have to because after a long time
> we have here visiting our
> very noticeable friend Beda Jedlička.[2]

Jirka went on to joke about Beda's size (he is indeed a large man) before finishing his stage talk. In the intimate confines of the Balbínka, Beda was able to respond from the back of the room to Jirka's mocking tribute to his presence with a halfhearted thanks that I picked up on my camera: "Děkuju, děkuju." The members of the band were already in their quartet-singing positions at this point, so Jirka continued the exchange by quipping across the microphone to mandolinist Tomáš Dvořák that since Beda had already thanked them, they didn't have to actually sing—"Už nemusíme!"

We in the audience laughed, knowing, as Tomáš did, that the song was still going to happen. After a quiet moment of preparation and expectation, banjoist Zbyněk Bureš intoned most of the stirring first line of the song:

> "There is a . . ."

Then there was silence again, a jarring pause this time, as Zbyněk suddenly stopped, ducking out of the tight arc of the quartet. The other three let out their pent-up breath with a mix of surprise, laughter, and indignation as he bent to fiddle with the PA mixer. We had all—audience *and* band—recovered from the interruption by the time he stood back up; Tomáš strummed C again, and the group began in earnest:

> There is a God and only one
> Who made the earth and sun
> He made all things, created man
> According to His plan.
>
> There is a God and He is real
> Deep in my heart His love I feel
> When I am laid beneath the sod
> I'll see and know there is a God
> There is a God.

The audience remained silent through the last fading note, then applauded wildly, nudging my recorder's sound meter into the red. Along with the power of the singing and the audience reaction, though, the preparation and setup leading to the performance caught my attention. As I will explain below, gospel material is usually set apart by a tone of reverence, if not an outright sermon. Jirka's earthy jab at Beda, Tomáš's quip, and Zbyněk's fussy attention to the sound equipment indicate a performative frame for this "gospel" song that differs greatly from many bluegrass settings in the United States.

I found out after the 2007 concert that a more specific issue about gospel songs was troubling this group, an issue of the members' personal convictions. While Zbyněk had made clear in conversations and interviews since 2003 that he was not a *věřící* (a [Christian] believer), gospel material had always been a part of Reliéf's repertory and central to their reputation as performers. While in my interactions with other members of the band I had noted the gap between what I perceived to be their personal beliefs and the theology embedded in the lyrics they sing as well as the quartet performance style that they emulate, I hadn't pursued the matter. Jirka Holoubek explained once that singing gospel music is "like playing for a Bach mass," a task that he performed during his formal training as a flutist. Though mandolinist Tomáš Dvořák had sung gospel songs with the group since the late 1990s, in the years leading up to the 2007 performance I describe above, he began voicing a more pointedly atheist stance, moving from indifference toward sacred lyrical content to direct opposition.

In an interview from the spring of 2008, Tomáš explained his problem in more detail, with reference to a classic gospel song recorded by the bluegrass group Doyle Lawson and Quicksilver:[3]

> to sing
> "what a wonderful change in my life
> has been wrought since Jesus came into my heart"
> three verses of this sentence
> it's quite hard
> this is not true
> not at all . . .
> I'm a kind of person that
> likes to do things
> REALLY
> and
> not lying
> like
> český opravdové
> so I don't want to go out with a girl
> and tell her that I love her
> when it is not true
> this is an example
> this is exactly what I am doing when I sing gospel.[4]

Tomas emphasized the world "really" as he spoke, and slipped from his serviceable English to use a Czech adjective meaning "real, genuine, earnest" as he emphasized his desire to sing truthfully, and not perform something with Reliéf that he doesn't personally believe. The effective power of Reliéf's performance, Tomáš's dissident stance, and my own experiences performing gospel material with members of the band lead me to argue that sharp divisions between the sacred and the secular might obscure a more complicated terrain of "in-between" spaces and performative expressions. As I pursued my questions, I discovered that concerns about gospel material were linked to seemingly incompatible senses of what is true—not just in musical presentation, but in the larger performance of life. This chapter focuses on the pragmatics of sensation, identification, and location that are involved in the playful but serious discourse in this particular part of "being Czech bluegrass."

PERFORMING BLUEGRASS GOSPEL

While bluegrass style and practice references and includes elements from the rural US heartlands, deserted by emigrants seeking jobs in urban areas, the music is largely what pioneering bluegrass scholar Robert Cantwell (1984, xi) calls a "representation" of older Appalachian music. As a key part of this representation, the musical work of the "father of bluegrass music," Bill Monroe, included a sacred element, the form of which indicates bluegrass's position between its rural roots and a growing urban audience during the 1960s and 1970s. This gospel component also reveals some of the tensions involved in performing sacred repertory in that "in-between" space—it involves a degree of playful/serious re-presentation in which performers and audiences accept something foreign or otherwise outside their identifying experiences.

Bill Monroe was born near Rosine, Kentucky, in the hardscrabble Pennyroyal region, yet when he constructed an image for his early 1940s band the Blue Grass Boys, he did not adopt a costume associated with the farming or coal areas of his home territory.[5] Monroe instead dressed his early bands in jodhpurs, starched shirts, short ties, and tasteful Stetson hats, an equestrian outfit that suggests a specific part of Kentucky, more to the east: the Bluegrass region, connected with horse racing and other high-class pursuits, associations that Monroe wished to use in legitimizing his music as a mainstream popular form.[6]

Monroe maintained tight conceptual control over the 150-odd musicians who served as "Blue Grass Boys" over the group's fifty-eight years of operation.[7] He used their particular gifts to color his evolving vision of bluegrass as a pop idiom, then as part of the folk revival, and finally as a central part of country music's history. These musicians paved the way for all the rest of us who have flocked to the music in the last half-century. We are able to join in the imaginative, albeit sometimes deceptive, play that Monroe initiated in bluegrass, and—as Czech musicians do—we can enjoy the possibilities for re-creation that the music affords.

Through the mid-1900s, Monroe borrowed material and styles from the growing field of southern gospel (Goff 2002) and other sacred sources and carefully inserted them into his stage show, well outside church worship experiences. The typical in-between role of gospel music is clear in the ways Monroe typically programmed it as part of his live shows . Monroe welded together the secular heat of "Saturday night" and the sacred poise of "Sunday morning" in the course of a single performance, carefully posing the two to preserve their performative effect as part of his traditionalist project. Monroe's performances with his band at the Bean Blossom Jamboree followed a strict pattern by which sacred repertory was carefully placed in the course of an evening's presentation—a special period known as "hymn time" that fell after the guest slot and before the big finale. Although usually a short segment (only one or two songs), it was, as bluegrass historian Neil Rosenberg (2005, 236) recounts, "always there."

Sacred material provided a respite from the high-energy drive of Monroe's stage show, which featured high-flying vocal and instrumental virtuosity. "[T]he religious aspects," Rosenberg (2005, 237) continues, "emphasized a traditional 'right' way (more important than individual style) and family-like integration with the group." During Monroe's "hymn time," the group joined sonic and spiritual unity: "All emphasis was placed on the total performance of the song in [a] reverent and ritualistic way; this is the hymn, it's treated seriously, nothing more need be said." Monroe's similar blend of elements in bluegrass gospel accomplishes a very different goal, however—his presentation of a sacred-traditional element would be accessible and intelligible not just to the rural core audience in which bluegrass originated, but also to disparate urban and even international audiences.

The current scene shows that gospel material persists in bluegrass practice, both on Saturday night and on Sunday morning. There are specialists: Doyle Lawson and Quicksilver are known in bluegrass circles for their sophisticated quartet arrangements, Jerry and Tammy Sullivan were known for their particular gospel message (Bernhardt 2001), and mainstream contemporary bluegrass stars Blue Highway received an IBMA award and a Grammy nomination for their 2003 album *Wondrous Love*, featuring that old hymn sung in a singing convention style very different from most bluegrass vocalism.[8] Bluegrass musicians of all stripes vie for the International Bluegrass Music Association's "Gospel Recorded Performance of the Year" award, and whole festivals are devoted to the sacred side of the music.[9]

There are a few performers who poke fun at the gospel side of bluegrass, but even these jests reinforce the importance of gospel singing as a genre-defining practice. The Steep Canyon Rangers' award-winning collaboration with comedian and banjoist Steve Martin produced an irreverent song proposing atheism as a gospel theme.[10] As a member of the fledgling Steep Canyon Rangers in 2001, however, I wrote a gospel song so that our first self-released album would emulate Monroe's practice of including a minimal amount of gospel material as part of our re-creation of bluegrass as a style.[11]

FOLK AND DOUBLEDNESS

Spirituál Kvintet was one of the most important groups in the foundational postwar period of Czech musical Americanism. While not a "bluegrass" or even a country group, the Kvintet was important for establishing a model for the reproduction of American repertory, especially sacred songs. With a debut in Prague in 1961, Spirituál Kvintet was one of the first Czech *folk* (Beckerman 1996) groups, wowing crowds with Czech and American traditional or folk-movement songs, as well as their trademark: African American spirituals and gospel songs (Vondrák and Skotal 2004, 67).

Through the sixties, Spirituál Kvintet was able to delve deeper into American musical culture, thanks to the liberalizing thaw of the Prague Spring leading up to 1968 and the scholarly work of bandleader/musicologist Jiři Tichota. The band's name indicates the importance of African American religious song to the performers and their audiences. The Kvintet's performances of songs like "Joshua Fit the Battle of Jericho" and "Swing Low" (both in Czech retextings and in the original English) were iconic as a soundtrack to the Czechoslovak 1960s.

Spirituál Kvintet's engagement with gospel material stands in contrast to the first "Czech bluegrass" band. The Greenhorns added a new genre to the growing Czech folk movement, becoming a popular group through the 1970s. Perhaps due to government pressure, the band rarely performed gospel material. A song of theirs with a melody resembling Hank Williams's "I Saw the Light" is the one tenuously gospel-related example I could find in their recorded works.[12] With a few exceptions (most notably Petr Kůs's groups Quintet and Blanket), most of the bands that followed the Greenhorns in re-creating bluegrass also followed their example in paying little attention to gospel songs until Zbyněk Bureš founded Reliéf in the mid-1990s.

RELIÉF'S BLUEGRASS GOSPEL

Zbyněk Bureš was raised in a "bluegrass home," a common background for Czechs whose parents grew up in the 1960s listening to Spirituál Kvintet and the Greenhorns. Zbyněk's father was a country and bluegrass fan so devoted to the music that he would rise in the morning to catch the 5:00 A.M. country show on US American Forces Network broadcasts, pulling in the sounds of America all the way from Munich and Luxembourg. Zbyněk described to me the posture during which he spent many childhood hours in the 1980s: lying in front of a record player listening to the Greenhorns and Marko Čermák's banjo, to tapes his father made of the AFN broadcasts, and (as time went on and access to recordings improved) to his father's collection of imported LP records.[13]

After initial study of the clarinet, Zbyněk settled on the banjo, and through the early 1990s he played with increasingly more skilled musicians. In his teenage years during this decade, he also began writing songs. His early output was mainly gospel *a cappella* songs: sacred texts paired with complicated three- and four-part vocal harmony arrangements. Zbyněk would write or adapt both the words and the music. When I questioned him about the reasons for his involvement with religious repertory, he replied that it had to do mainly with the singing style:

> I was very, very interested in quartet singing
> and in bluegrass the quartet singing is almost exclusively . . .
> joined with gospels
> with some exceptions
> like Flatt and Scruggs
> when it comes to quartet singing
> it's ninety-nine percent gospel.[14]

By 1997 the group had solidified in its current form: Zbyněk on banjo, Dobro, and pedal steel guitar, Tomáš Dvořák on mandolin, Jirka Holoubek on guitar, and Pavel Peroutka on bass. While Zbyněk plays a central vocal role, the others all take a turn leading songs. Few Czech bands today can rival Reliéf's combination of vocal and instrumental virtuosity, as all of the members are hot pickers as well as polished singers. Yet as Tomáš Dvořák ruefully told me, as spectacular as the rest of their stage show can be, the gospels remain their most popular material—even among listeners outside the bluegrass community:

> when some people who doesn't—
> don't know bluegrass
> come to our concert to see us
> so
> most of them
> ninety-nine percent of them

these people
will say
"ok it was good, especially the a cappella singing"
"the banjo and so on, it was good too" . . .
"but I prefer the a cappella, these gospels"
everybody says this.[15]

Reliéf continued to oblige audiences who called for gospel material. At the November 2007 concert I discuss above, the band performed twenty-nine songs, seven of which were gospel songs. Tomáš's concerns about the gospels were coming to a head during my fieldwork year in 2007–2008, and when I interviewed him and Zbyněk, changes were in the works.

TRANSITION AND TRUTH

Anthropologist Gerald Creed (1998) joins Sharad Chari and Katherine Verdery (Chari and Verdery 2008) and other scholars of postsocialism in questioning the notion of transition, focusing instead on the details of daily life, finding what he calls "a moving testimony to the power of everyday practice to reconfigure the very conditions that inform it" (3). Sociologist Michael Burawoy (1999, 309), in theorizing on the future of postsocialist studies, is similarly critical of "transition," fearing that scholars who follow this model might "lose sight of alternatives . . . novel lenses through which to interpret the present and the past, as well as the future." Perhaps, he muses, "native" theory will arise from within the former Eastern Bloc, and "a new generation of dissidents [will] abandon the optimism and teleology of so-called transitology and turn to something more akin to postcolonial theory" (309–310).

The idea of local practice as a contestation with global forces emerged when I spoke with Ondra Holoubek, brother of Reliéf's guitar player Jirka Holoubek, about the gospel song issue. In talking with him one night after the band's performance at the Balbínka in 2007, I learned that he felt strongly that performing gospel material compromised the group's artistic integrity. Ondra's idea of concentrated personal work as a way of domesticating a foreign form and integrating it into the local group discourse resonates not only with the scholars I cite above, but with the local Czech experience of communism and the post-1989 transition, as well as with ideas of art and truth.

Ondra Holoubek is a master luthier who builds mandolins and guitars based on early twentieth-century US models, mainly—as is the case with many other present-day luthiers—Gibson mandolins and Martin guitars. His

Ondra Holoubek in his workshop, Louňovice, Czech Republic, 2016.

work closely parallels that of Reliéf, and is of comparable quality in terms of mastery and innovation with regard to borrowed American forms.

In our conversations, Ondra compared his practice of lutherie with Reliéf's "dramaturgy," as he put it—their performance choices, and particularly their choice of repertory. He accuses them of slavishly following the bluegrass community (in the Czech Republic, the United States, and the world) by continuing to perform gospel material. Privileging authorship over emulation, Ondra insists that the members of Reliéf are capable of better things than rote reproduction of quartet arrangements, and that the "gospel" material is holding them back from more truthful artistic expression, and thus wider success as a band. As he put it,

> These guys [Reliéf]
> should realize
> they aren't just some little band screwing around
> but that they have strength . . .
> that is in authorship

and these things
and that is what makes the band work . . .
it's from within
within these people.[16]

By connecting them with universal virtues (musicianship, creativity), Ondra insists that the members of Reliéf are capable of transcending the narrow bluegrass microcommunity where they operate, and the Czech region where they live and work—and perhaps even the sense of being "small" that comes along with both these identifications. Anthropologist Ladislav Holý (1996) explains the common Czech idea of the "small Czech" (*malý český člověk*) in contrast to the "Great Czech Nation." Individuals, he argues (always *other* Czechs) are often considered resentful, petty, and possibly larcenous, while the Czech nation as a whole is literate, artistic, noble, and brave (77)—the character traits that Ondra attributes to Reliéf. The small Czech is an ambiguous figure, often exhibiting stereotypical traits that Czechs sometimes love and sometimes love to hate. Gospel songs seem to involve a similar balance of self-praise and self-critique—strands that Ondra weaves into discussion of his music-related work.

Ondra builds bluegrass-type instruments—two of which are used by the members of Reliéf: Tomáš's mandolin and Jirka's guitar. Thus for Ondra the band and their performance of gospel songs tie into larger problems of integrity that he confronts in his own work. Ondra is concerned that his brother and Reliéf are not expressing themselves truthfully, a move that might profit them artistically and in terms of success. At one point while we were talking, Ondra pointed to a mandolin body on the workbench behind him, saying that he had stopped work on the instrument because the ribs were too thin. He could have continued, and sold it for 80,000 Czech crowns (approximately $5,000 in US dollars at the time), but he laid it aside "because it wasn't just right." Likewise, he insists, Reliéf should leave the gospel songs behind, because they are able to do material that is at the same time more complex, more rooted in their actual life experiences, and that will represent them better in the music business, as well as being more artistically satisfying to them, to other Czechs who are not a part of the small bluegrass scene, and perhaps to larger audiences of the global musical scene.

TOWARD "LIVING IN TRUTH"

Ondra echoes a Czech discourse on "truthfulness" in daily life and work that is rooted in the years of communist primacy in the former Czechoslovakia. In his 1971 essay "The Power of the Powerless," Czech dissident author and ethicist Vaclác Havel imagines a greengrocer who follows the government's expectations by hanging a sign in his shop window that repeats a typical communist slogan, "Workers of the World, Unite!"—not because of enthusiasm for the communist system, but because of his desire to live in peace. His natural desire to live undisturbed leads to complicity with the system, a falsehood that Havel calls "living in a lie" (1989, 41).

The "lie" that Reliéf perform through singing words that speak to a faith they don't possess is, after a fashion, a postsocialist complication of Havel's example. Concerns about the figurative and literal "loss of self" that Havel outlines are not limited to the communist situation in which he lived and wrote. The Czech Republic separated from Slovakia just over three years after the end of Communist single-party rule, and is now negotiating its new political identity as part of the European Union, the North Atlantic Treaty Organization, and other spheres of power and influence. Meanwhile, Czechs are adjusting to the pressures of a market economy and the arrival of globalized corporate consumerism. Ladislav Holý (1996, 138–167) concludes that in the post-1989 Czech sociopolitical landscape, concerns over both definitions of "Czechness" and the individual selfhood of Czechs are as immediate and messy as they were during the socialist period.

In refusing to sing some gospel material, Reliéf's doubting mandolinist Tomáš shows that tensions around the performance of truth remain alive among Czechs. His concerns call into question not only the practice of gospel singing, but—as Ondra reminds us—the whole endeavor of re-creating American bluegrass-related music. The members of Reliéf are grappling with a variety of ideas about what the performance of *American* gospel songs means—they operate in a globalized discourse of what bluegrass is and should be (the shadow of Bill Monroe—and his strict shaping of the music—loom large here), as well as local discourses about how the music intersects with issues of aesthetics and belief.

Ondra Holoubek's rhetoric of "craftsmanship" echoes philosopher and statesman Tomáš Garrigue Masaryk's proposal of *práce drobná* ("detailed work") as a path toward rebuilding the creativity and confidence of Czechs in the twilight of the Habsburg Empire. Philosopher Roger Scruton (1988, 116) expands on Masaryk's idea of detailed work and links it to Havel's writing, emphasizing the social conscience of this practice: "In place of the great totalitarian schemes we have only small-scale work—*práce drobná*—which permits us to strive for the improvement of our situation, while remaining obedient to the moral law." The concept of *práce drobná* fits with the sustained, concentrated efforts that many Czech bluegrass participants undertake in their pursuit of the music, suggesting that Czech re-creations of bluegrass are examples of domestication as intense as those that Creed describes.

Linguistic anthropologist Alexei Yurchak's (2006) critique of black-and-white distinctions between dissidence and complicity in late twentieth-century Soviet-style socialism calls into question the distinction between truth and lies made by dissidents like Havel (1989) and Solzhenitsyn (2004). Yurchak's elaboration on the Russian idea of *vnye* outlines a sense of simultaneous "inside-outsideness" similar to the "in-betweenness" that I have observed in Czech performances of bluegrass and their negotiation of the tensions between "Czech" and "American." Gospel singing filtered through the persisting atmosphere of *vnye* would afford a singer like Tomáš Dvořák the in-between space to be both convinced and skeptical of the musical and lyrical content in sacred material.

MAKING GOSPEL WORK IN THE CZECH CONTEXT

As I mention above, Tomáš Dvořák told me in 2008 that he had begun to resist performing sacred material with Reliéf because he doesn't personally agree with the Christian texts. Following, in a way, Ondra Holoubek's wish that the group could be truer to their "Czechness" and to Ondra's artistic-philosophical ideals, Tomáš began to flatly reject songs with texts requiring him to sing about an intense personal experience of faith. He is also conscientious about the effect of his decision on the performing life of the group, however. "I made a compromise," he told me in our interview:

> I told the other guys
> ok
> let's do some gospels
> but some neutral . . .
> like
> if it's a Bible story
> then, ok
> it's a part of my culture
> then this is definitely ok for me.[17]

Tomáš resolves the tension by accepting biblical stories as part of a shared cultural heritage.

In my observations during my fieldwork since 2007, Reliéf have held to Tomáš's proposal, apart from exceptions such as the example that opens this chapter. To fill the resulting holes in their concert set lists, they began to perform more of Zbyněk Bureš's original songs—indeed, drawing on the "authorship" that Ondra Holoubek insists is one of their chief creative assets. Zbyněk used to write gospel songs that covered both "neutral" material and "personal faith" themes, but these days his writing is based not in gospel-type narratives, but in personal experiences as well as creative musings on love and alienation inspired by modern literature and poetry.

Speaking with Tomáš in an interview, I tried to get him to specify why gospel songs of "personal faith" disagreed with him. Two themes emerged: Firstly, Tomáš didn't want people in the audience to think that he was a Christian. For my part, as a practicing Christian, I can understand his distaste—institutional Christianity does not have the most attractive reputation and public image in the Czech Republic, or in the United States. Yet I was surprised at the second reason: Tomáš was concerned that performing this music was actually effectively performing some aspect of religious faith. In talking about performance of gospels, he said:

> It gives something to the people
> to Christians
> they take something else from this song
> than I give on it
> and
> it's like
> [pause]
> it's quite difficult to explain
> for me it's hard to sing about something that says nothing to me
> even [though] I know that people understand it a different way than me.[18]

I agree with him on this point about function and efficacy. I have participated in performances by this band in ways that were decidedly religious. For example, their performance of the song "There Is a God" has long been a favorite of mine because of the way it joins a simple, almost forceful statement of belief to a musical setting that builds the words into glorious blooms of sound. Their performance expresses faith in a way that resonates with my beliefs, and my musical sensibility, connecting them in a powerful way. The power of the performance does not seem to be inherent to the text, or even the musical performance of the text/song on its own. I suspect that the performance setting is a large part of the experience I describe here.

While working at home on a conference presentation based on this research, I played for the first time a live recording of Reliéf singing "There Is a God" through the stereo system I had just set up at my desk. The first verse came out softly—audibly, but only just so. In that moment I wondered, "Is this performance really worth playing for the folks at the Society for Ethnomusicology? It doesn't sound like much." It was only when I corrected for the low output of my computer and turned the volume dial nearly to its limit that I really heard it—the grinding of voice on voice, not just knowing that they are singing in close harmony, but feeling that process of "singing close" in my ears, in an electric sizzle down my neck and into that familiar warm resonance in my chest—that was it! As ethnomusicologist Gage Averill (2003, 178) states, when it happens in the right way, when it works, there can be something more, "something different," about quartet singing. Talking about his experiences singing with Bill Monroe, Peter Rowan concretized this "something" as "a strange overtone . . . almost a buzz rather than a note" that sounds between his voice and Monroe's (Cantwell 1984, 212).

The intimacy of the experiences I describe here—listening to the music on a high-fidelity stereo and in the Balbínka's cozy listening room—serves to heighten the effects of quartet singing. Perhaps this is part of Tomáš's strong reactions about singing songs he doesn't believe—he is accountable not only to himself, but to the circle of people who share the transcendent experience of Reliéf's singing. Perhaps, to use Richard Schechner's (1985, 130) terms, Tomáš fears that Reliéf's performances are not just "transporting," but also somehow "transforming."

The bodily dispositions involved in gospel singing make it difficult to separate the medium from the message of this music form. Many participants and observers attest that there is something special about sacred quartet singing and the ways, as Averill (2003, 178) puts it, that this expression creates a particular version of Steven Feld's (1984) metaphor that considers "sound structure as social structure." This sort of experience not only blurs the line between performer and audience; it suggests complicated blends of Schechner's concepts of "transforming" and "transporting." All of us who have heard Reliéf in the Balbínka club (or who experience the sounds on record and remember or imagine live performances) are taken up in the musical experience, share it, and then settle back down (Schechner 1985). Resonating with their quartet sound, we are squeezed into the matrix of their close-harmony sound and swept up into an intimate musical experience. The shadows of our actual location fade, and we rest in a perfectly harmonized territory of concord before returning to "normal" space like the Balbínka, or my messy office.

And yet the potential for "transformation" in the gospel material Reliéf sings still troubles me, as it does Tomáš. It took an experience of my own to drive home the ways that Czech performances of gospel songs can be truthful and transformative within the "as-if" and in-between territory of Czech bluegrass.

SINGING UNBELIEF

My singing moment happened on a trip outside of Prague in May 2008. I had traveled with Zbyněk Bureš and his friend Svatka Štěpánková to the town of Kašperské Hory, a few hours' drive southwest of Prague in the Šumava mountain range, which separates Bohemia from southern Germany. The morning after we arrived, we went for a walk, and ended up at the Church of Saint Nicholas (Svatý Mikuláš) on the outskirts of town, a graveyard chapel built in the early fourteenth century. The elderly caretaker gave Svatka the keys, and we let ourselves in. The dusty sanctuary glowed as the morning sunlight filtered onto worn pews, baroque carvings, and a partially disassembled organ. Our voices hushed, and the clanking of the huge keys echoed invitingly. Zbyněk snapped his fingers, appraising the acoustics.

I was itching to make music with these people whom I had heard play and sing only on stage, to feel from within the glow that gospel singing could have in the Czech context. We hadn't had a good jam the night before; we were tired from traveling, and the setting and mood just hadn't been right. But in the church that morning, we stepped into a space that asked us to fill it with song. As we stood on the verge of singing, the appropriate material soon

Zbyněk Bureš exploring the Svatý Mikuláš church in Kašperské Hory, Czech Republic, 2008.

presented itself: Zbyněk asked if we wanted to sing "Amazing Grace," a song that he likes to perform with a local Šumava group of bluegrass jammers.

The impromptu recording I made with my digital camcorder shows that we audibly floundered a bit before finding our vocal parts and the right words. As we pushed our lines and tones into alignment, however, the spaces of the church building lifted and blended our voices, carrying them farther than we could have taken them ourselves. This singing was, and remains in my memory, an experience that was shockingly intimate and moving. Shocking, to me, because it was a musical, not a religious, experience. While I was singing, I wasn't thinking about the lyrical content of the song "Amazing Grace," but about these people I was singing with, being with them in music. It wasn't about words outlining Christian faith, but it was about people being together.

Putting this together afterward, I was taken aback. "Amazing Grace" is a song that has been significant in my life; it is a joining of words and music that has supported and encouraged me in joining my faith and daily life for a long time. Thus it strikes me as a bit odd that I "went native" for a moment, slipping into an engagement with "Amazing Grace" that was musical and not my usual religious one. This moment reverses an experience that Deidre Sklar (1994, 17) describes having in the course of her fieldwork among practitioners of a New Mexico Catholic form of devotion. She had a moment of connection, if not to the object of Christian worship (God), then to the process and experience of worship that her believing colleagues experienced. During the hubbub of a festival day, she was shuffled through a crowd and into a line that drew her into a chapel, where, with no other alternative, she simply followed the movements of those around her, and knelt before the altar. There, "the combination of descending to my knees and feeling an enlivened connection to the figure depicted in the image gave me a taste of the experience whose expression I had been studying."

Like Sklar, I had my personal convictions contradicted, or perhaps simply redirected, as I engaged bodily with Czech musician colleagues. Of course, this is not an unusual trajectory for ethnographers of religion, and of religious music especially. Jeff Titon's work has led him to many borderlands between scholarship, music, and belief. Writing about participating with Old Regular Baptists in scholarly bimusical engagement, Titon (1995, 296) describes himself singing, relating, learning, but not believing their brand of theology. When asked, "How can you sing with them when you don't believe as they do?" Titon counters: "I think I believe in music as they do." Titon's "musical experience" was "indeed spiritual," but it "transcended the particularities of any denomination or doctrine."

But can religious music's spiritually enlivening power be nullified by an unbelieving interpretation of it? On this point, I disagree with Tomáš. I am left with a feeling that there is a spiritual dimension to gospel singing—precisely because the power of this specific sort of musical experience can bring people together across significant boundaries, such as the transcendent musical experience that Titon describes.[19] The musical moment I shared in the Šumava church blurred my observer/participant boundary, bridged language and other cultural divides, brushed aside for a moment the complex history that distinguishes Czech from US bluegrass, and crossed any number of other boundary lines that might have intersected our singing group that morning. The persisting resonances of this singing moment challenge my instinct to separate along the normal boundaries, and offer wider understandings that might not separate "sacred" from "secular," but acknowledge that the two are seldom all that separate.

WORK, PLAY, AND BELIEF

When I first approached Tomáš Dvořák and asked for an interview during the spring of 2008, he suggested that we talk in his car as we rode to a band rehearsal. It wasn't as noisy as I expected, and Tomáš's station wagon turned out to be a relaxed place to talk. As we rolled along between Prague and Brno, I tried to keep the interview focused on his thoughts on the subject of singing gospel songs, but in the process we both shared a lot of our convictions about performance, truthfulness, and so on. Highway driving allowed a flow of conversation, but just as our discussion turned to the problems of performing sacred repertory when a musician is not a believer, we had to navigate secondary roads. At the most sensitive point of the interview—discussion of the issue I was most concerned with—we were both trying to make out road signs in the rainy twilight. This added, I think, to the tone of urgency in Tomáš's comments about "truth" and "lying" that I quote above.

After successfully locating the stretch of road leading to our destination, Tomáš collected his thoughts as I tried to find a way to end the interview gracefully after the crescendo of emotion that our discussion had sparked. Looking back, I think I was trying to resolve his negotiations with Reliéf over sacred repertory, to find a way to make sense of the tangled issues of identity and performance that confront Czech bluegrassers. Tomáš backed away a bit from his earlier stance that he can't sing gospel material he doesn't believe in:

> but I
> the other side
> I must say that I really enjoy

singing the gospels with Reliéf
because of the harmonies
and because it works.[20]

The musical performance of gospel material in the Czech Republic does "work." It is sustainable, despite being out of place, both in geography and in terms of belief. I suggest that this efficacy is wrapped up with the "sacred" and "secular" in something serious: the dynamic of play as theorized by Huizinga (1955), Turner (1982), and other scholars. My intersecting theomusicological conviction (Spencer 1994) that divine joy in unbounded "play" is at the root of human creativity echoes the work of theologians such as Jeremy Begbie. From this standpoint, I consider play as a possibly important part of a "deep" (Geertz 2000) and even an "ultimate" concern. Paul Tillich (1957, 52) argues that a disciplined atheist stance (such as that taken by Tomáš) reflects a concern with the "ultimate," and is a sort of faith "even if the act of faith includes the denial of God." Thus I perceive a profound integrity in the musicality and the play of Reliéf's gospel singing.[21]

The avocational work of "play" is serious in the Czech Republic, and Reliéf's members were continuing a rich legacy of amateurism. Despite their professionalism as performers, they all had day jobs, which included audiology researcher, radio moderator, chemistry technician, and music teacher. That they did not derive their principal income from playing with this band allowed them flexibility, particularly in what engagements they agreed to do, how many times they performed, and the sorts of material they chose to play.

Tomáš Dvořák with Reliéf at the Balbínka, November 2007.

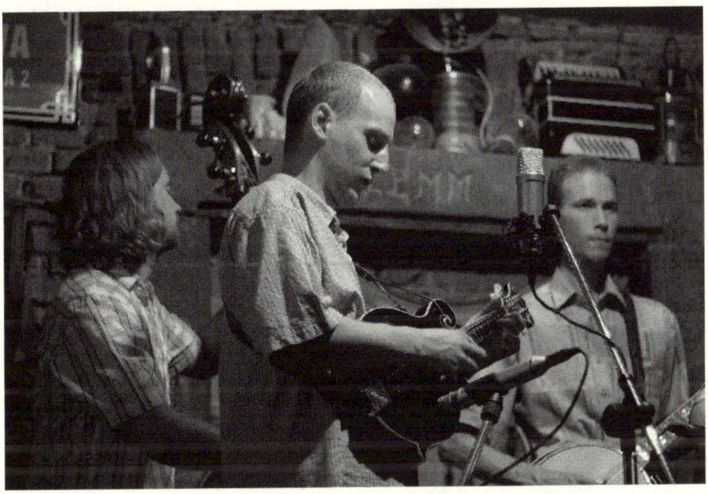

As I portray Czech bluegrassers nudging at the boundaries between "work" and "play," "American" and "Czech," "sacred" and "secular," the quotation marks multiply and my writing work itself becomes a species of play. For better or worse, ethnomusicology these days seems to require a lot of this sort of scare-quote play—implying the weight of a word like "authenticity" but holding back from full commitment to its semantic weight. My fieldwork, as my wife, Emily, likes to playfully tell people, was just a lot of "playing with Czechs"—a lot of musical performance and interactive pleasure. But in the "field," as here in front of my computer, there were plenty of interruptions, cracks, and interstices of experience where work and play mixed.

On the evening of Reliéf's performance at the Balbínka that I describe at the beginning of this chapter, Jirka Holoubek introduced me, telling the audience about my background and history in the Czech Republic, and called me to the microphone to explain *why* I was in Prague, and what exactly I was doing for my "work." He used the word *práce*, which in Czech, like the English word "work," can refer either to employment or to something written, such as a *disertační práce* (dissertation). He didn't press the issue all that long, but he did get all of us laughing about the fact that I was there that evening *pracovně* ("workingly") while playing the fiddle. Moments such as these indicate that Czech bluegrassers *know* the play they are engaged in, and accept the oddness that my work is based in our play, as they accept the persisting, distinct, and somewhat unusual Czechness of their own endeavors. We proceed undeterred because, as Tomáš reminds us, "it works."

While intercultural tangles might seem to undermine the full sung power of a song like "Amazing Grace" or "There Is a God," through processes of Czech bluegrass play these circumstances instead become a rich context for eloquently moving musical performance and the chance to ask tough questions about the ethics of performance choices and style such as those that Tomáš poses.

In introducing his essay on the ambiguity of play, Brian Sutton-Smith (2006, 297) contrasts Gregory Bateson's (1955) observation about animals at play, that they "bite each other playfully, knowing that the playful nip connotes a bite, but not what a bite connotes," with Richard Schechner's (1988) rejoinder, that while "a playful nip is not a bite, it is also *not* not a bite." Following this tangled mode of talking about "play," I could insist that Czech bluegrass gospel singing is *not* not religious music making. At the same time, though, it is *not* not American just as it is *not* not Czech; it is *not* not secular just as it is *not* not sacred. In the end, these labels and prescriptions seem less important than the faithful, truthfully slippery, yet powerfully effective music making that defies them all.

A TAG: AMERICA/*AMERIKA*

While some performances of bluegrass songs end with an abrupt chop on the final tonic chord, damping the resonance of the instruments, other endings allow the continuing ringing strings to fade the song out. Often a vocal number will end on the song's chorus, with a repetition of the last line. These "tag" lines are often the title of the song, and, hanging in the air at the end of a performance, are also iconic articulations of many of the central themes of bluegrass, of place, community, loss, and desire: "I wonder where you are tonight"; "I wonder if she ever thinks of me"; "Why did I leave the plow in the field and look for a job in the town?"

Sometimes a song's tag line will produce a shift in the meaning of the chorus, offering a zinger ending that opens new space for meaning even as the song ends. Petr Kůs's song "Zlatá rybka" (The golden fish) features such a turn. I first heard the song when Ralph Schut was invited to join Reliéf on stage at the Malostranská Beseda when I saw them in the spring of 2000. At that time I didn't understand the text at all, but I was fascinated to see this Dutch person so fluently convey the story and sense of the song—his effectiveness was clear when the audience responded with cheers. Later I enjoyed hearing Ralph sing lead vocals, conveying the song just as effectively as part of Kůs's own band, Fámy, in 2006.[1]

The setting for this song is the old fairytale in which a fisherman's encounters with a magical fish lead him to wish for material wealth (first a new net and boat, and eventually a golden palace), but his greed begins to irritate the fish, who then returns him to his original net, boat, and occupation. The chorus changes with each iteration, highlighting what the fisherman gains at that stage in the story: first a golden fish, then a golden palace, and then, in the third and final verse, his old boat and net. Kůs's ending, instead of following convention and repeating verbatim the final line, "Starou lod' a starou sít' zas máš" (You have your old boat and net again), adds a slightly different tag to underline the vainness of the fisherman's strivings: "Starou lod' a starou sít' v rukou máš" (You have your old boat and net in your hand). The twist in this extended line is underscored by a deceptive cadence that prolongs the ending. Many of the Czechs who sing this song follow Kůs in holding the last syllable of the line on a subdominant (IV) chord before finally returning to the tonic (I), highlighting the message that appreciating what you have is better than wishing for more.

In addition to underlining the idea of the song that precedes it, the "tag" also indicates to the audience that it is time to react to that segment of the performance, to applaud, shout, whistle, or yell out requests for favorite songs. As I leave readers to consider their responses to this volume, I present two cases of the desire to be close to, or the desire to reproduce elements of, Americanness—cases where the people concerned fulfilled their desires by choosing things and places that are *Czech*.

"AMERICA ALL AROUND"

After meeting Marko Čermák when he agreed to an interview in 2008, I came to respect him not only for his historic role in the foundation of Czech bluegrass, but for the way he has dealt with his position as a subcultural celebrity. I also learned that his notoriety resulted not only from his musical work.

Marko obtained his official work credentials as a musician, but he started his working career in visual art. He gained a great deal of exposure as the illustrator of the "Rychlé šípy" adventure stories by Jaroslav Foglar.[2] He was in his seventies when I met him, and used his leisure time to draw and paint in his cabin in the Brdy woods when the weather wasn't right for canoeing on nearby rivers; winters found him at the foot of a ski resort where his wife taught lessons, living in a rebuilt trailer that he called his "winter den" (Čermák 2010, xxv).

Speaking with Marko led me to develop my ideas about Americanness, considering the ways that Czechs create, reshape, and use it for their own ends. He acknowledges the fantasy of Czech Americanism, but insists that it has real power. Following up on this theme during one of our interviews,

Marko Čermák approaching his cabin in the Udoli Děsu tramp settlement outside the village of Hatě, Czech Republic, 2011.

I asked him about his thoughts on traveling to the actual United States, and his answer surprised me:

> Since the beginning I've wanted terribly to go
> I wrote that I'd have crawled there on all fours . . .
> But we have dreamed up this America, that it is some kind of paradise . . .
> a paradise of music; that there are those cowboys; that there are those
> Indians . . .
> I illustrated these sorts of books and the texts, I wrote a lot of texts . . .
> And we dreamed up this romantic world
> and now my friends have started to travel there
> and they show their videos where there are highways
> you know, and highways, and highways, and these hotels . . .[3]

He gestured with disgust in talking about the actual situations of travel that would be necessary for him to visit the storied parts of the United States that inform his Americanist romance.

These impressions convey a depressing image of America. Čermák describes travel in the United States in ways that suggest the visions frozen by Edward Hopper and others who have captured the bleak roadside drabness of America. In her many trips to the US, Marko's friend Lilly Pavlak has seen plenty of "the road," traveling with bands and other bluegrassers. When she visited my home in the fall of 2009, she commented on the fact that my family didn't drive as much as many Americans that she had visited. I took her to the campus of UNC-Chapel Hill, where she continued this commentary, chuckling at seeing the students rushing to and from classes on foot: "I've never seen so many Americans walking before."

An automobile-dominated vision of the United States of America does not fit with the rhapsodic Czech romanticism of "Amerika" out of which Marko Čermák has made his career. As a musician, a songwriter, an illustrator for adventure stories, and a painter of landscapes, he has helped create the Czech romance with imagined ideals of the United States. In his vision of the US, a saddled horse, a canoe, or a covered wagon would be preferable.

Marko has successfully marketed many of his performances and songs using old-fashioned and rustic imagery based in ideas of the American West. In addition to his illustrations for stories, he has provided drawings of cowboys, instruments, and related musical-western imagery for songbooks, like the songbook entitled *Country zpěvník II* (Macek 2001). Not all Czechs enjoy the kind of sustained success in Americanism that Marko enjoys. Three of the fiddlers that I interviewed no longer focus on playing the bluegrass style. The bands Roll's Boys and Reliéf no longer perform publicly, and have let their websites lapse.[4] Zdeněk Roh remains proud that progressive banjo icon Tony Trischka owns an instrument he made. In August 2016, however, the Deering Banjo Company began marketing a new Trischka signature model; Zdeněk does not have the resources to mount a competing campaign.[5]

Still, almost all of the people featured in this volume persist in their Americanist projects. Zdeněk Roh still builds banjos, and plans trips to the United States when he has an opportunity to bring an instrument to an American customer. After years of participation in his local Indianist group, he now owns his own canvas teepee and a truck large enough to transport it to the sites where his group camps for several weeks a year. While Jindra Matuška and Honza Čermák are no longer part of Rakovnickej Potok, Jindra still continues to build banjos.[6] The former members of Reliéf play with an array of other bluegrass and country music bands. Slávka Franclíková spent a number of years working in New Zealand, during which time her posts to social media showed that she played there with a bluegrass band.[7]

The second case I will focus on here includes different dynamics involving personal dreams and motivations. Brothers Ralph and Chris Schut, Dutch by birth, are now residents of the Czech Republic—they moved there because of music, but are now enmeshed in larger networks. Choices made by Ralph in particular confirm Marko's estimation of the value of Czech Americanism. Christened Ralph Christian Friedrich Martin Schut (after the famous nineteenth-century luthier who founded C. F. Martin and Company), he grew up in a "bluegrass household" in the Netherlands. His father, Dennis, was a bluegrass aficionado; he played guitar (on a short-term basis) for US bluegrass performers Charlie Moore and Jim Eanes, and founded the band Spruce Pine in the late 1970s.

Ralph moved to the Czech Republic to study, and found a job soon after. He since started a family, living in his wife's hometown, Žďár nad Sázavou, not far from where we met playing in Roll's Boys and in other configurations in the circle around Zdeněk Roh. Chris followed his brother's lead, and as of 2016 was working as a sound engineer for the Czech bluegrass-related band Druhá Tráva. Both Schut brothers have found ways to live and work within the amateur and professional spheres of the Czech bluegrass world, enjoying the fruits of decades of Czech Americanism that Marko helped foster. These two immigrants have become part of the concerted Czech effort to cultivate bluegrass in the heart of Europe—as have I. Our interest is proof of the prominence that the Czech scene holds in Europe and beyond.

Marko's perspective sums up the sorts of imaginative and practical work that forms the pragmatic framework (the "reasons why") supporting bluegrass-related choices like those that the Schuts and I have made. Czech musicians find ways to draw sounds and style from the internet and—in Jan Čermák's words—from their heart. They weigh issues of fidelity and faith as they reproduce American songs and create their own bluegrass canons. Working both at home and abroad, they find ways to parlay their passion into avocations and careers.

Czechs' imagined versions of "Amerika" are often, as Marko told me in 2011, a *velká romantika*, a great romance that comes not from a desire to make money or grab at fame; it is something that comes from the heart.[8] During our 2008 interview, however, Marko went even further. Returning to the topic of visiting the United States, he used the Czech word *Amerika* to refer both to the US and to the forest clearing where we stood.

> . . . but that [United States of] America is normal and isn't as we dreamed it up
> And this dream I want to keep it. You know what I mean? . . .
> I could have been in America many times, even by invitation . . .
> Things there were worked out for me.
> But I wanted to keep for myself—I wanted to keep the impression of this beautiful, dreamed-up, unreal America . . .
> I am surrounded by this America—America is everywhere here, and here America.[9]

Marko's cabin, "El Toro," as it existed in 1926, with tramp musicians in the doorway holding a mandolin and guitar.

With these last words, Marko gestured around with his arm, imbuing the forest around the table where we sat with new significance. He had just explained that the cabin where we were meeting was a tramping shelter in the 1920s, and he showed me a faded black-and-white photograph of the structure with early twentieth-century tramps posing proudly in front of it.

Like many Czechs I have met, Marko is aware of the constructedness of Czech imaginings of America, and how they have become real in Czech practices. He prefers to keep[10] and cultivate his imagined America, even if it doesn't always harmonize with the *real* United States. The conceptions and constructions of *Amerika* that I have outlined in this volume are as varied as the *vono* that bluegrassers strive to embody in their music making.

Czechs sometimes carry out their bluegrass-related dreams—and also experience failures and frustrations as they undertake Americanist projects. In this respect, they are not that different from bluegrassers in the United States. In closing, I emphasize that the flourishing of bluegrass in Europe does not negate its continuing popularity in the genre's traditional heartland (or, for that matter, anywhere else). Considering how and why it is adopted elsewhere might give us pause, however, when we encounter claims for geographic or cultural boundaries around bluegrass. As I stood outside Marko's cabin interviewing him that day in 2008, I took in the rich greenery of this tranquil spot that has served as an Americanist retreat for nearly a century, listening to the creek, the birds, and Marko's thoughtful musings. In that moment, it made sense that America would be all around—beautiful, frustrating, imagined, and unreal—in the heart of Europe.

NOTES ON LANGUAGE

Transformations

The Czech-English language interaction constitutes one major venue for the intercultural drama of Czech bluegrass. I will not include here a detailed explanation of how the language is written and pronounced, but this brief summary will illustrate some relevant cases. Readers seeking a broader outline can refer to Johnston's (2008) excellent language explanations in the introductory material to his dissertation, as well as to more specialized and extensive grammar and usage texts such as those by Heim (1982) and Kresin et al. (2000)—and the description of informal/spoken Czech by Townsend (1990).

Czech grammar involves a wide array of transformations. When I first began to study the language, the lists of endings at the back of my textbook were intimidating. In Czech (as in Latin, German, Russian, and other inflected languages), these endings are attached to root words depending on their role and their relationship to other parts of speech. There are seven grammatical cases, each of which requires a special set of endings depending on gender (masculine, feminine, or neuter), number, and other factors.

There are many cultural borrowings and adaptions perceptible at the vocabulary level of the language. Due to the shifting regimes Czechs have lived under, their language is often cosmopolitan; adoptions of foreign words are common. In addition to domesticating the language through adding grammatical endings, Czechs often adapt words by respelling them using Czech phonography. For instance, *reportáž* is the Czech equivalent of the French word "reportage," and *džiny* is Czech for "jeans." The letter *c* as used in the English language leads to more complicated cases of adoption. The Czech pronunciation of *c* has a sound similar to *ts*, such that

English "hard *c*" sounds (whether *c* alone or the *ck* cluster) have no direct analog, and are typically written by Czechs as *k*. However, this transformation is not fully consistent, especially with the word "country," which is usually spelled like the original English word but pronounced as if the first letter were a *k*. Some common music style/genre designations create awkward situations for Czechs seeking to reconcile a foreign word with their native language. "Rock" is usually left as is, but the adjective form can become *rokový* (as in "rock music"). Country music also creates a problem, especially in the sonically alliterative but orthographically clashing (at least in Czech) phrase that refers to classic country: *klasický country*. These labels ("rock" and "country" especially) have been in oral circulation long enough that their usage in Czech is naturalized—by which I mean that Czechs seem so used to them that they don't note these as inconsistencies in their normally very consistent language.

In listening carefully to Czechs speaking and singing in English, I have noted a few of their most common mispronunciations. One of the most difficult sounds is *th*, which is entirely foreign to Czech speech and is often simplified into something like *dh* (thus the English word "weather" when spoken by a Czech often sounds like "wedder"). Vowel sounds are sometimes transformed. The slight twanging sound of *a* when followed by *n* (as in "pan" or "hand") is typically pushed too far up, and a bit toward the back of the mouth so that these words sound, to my ear, like "pen" and "hend." "Banjo," which of course is a central word in bluegrass discourse, is—per the typical Czech transformation—pronounced (and sometimes written) as *bendžo*.

Czech orthography is ultra-logical, which some observers attribute to the fact that Czech was resurrected in the mid-nineteenth century after centuries in which the official language of the area was German, the language of the Habsburg (and Austro-Hungarian) Empire.[1] Some theories hold that this rationalized resurrection normalized Czech pronunciation; in my experience as a language learner, this proves true: Czech vowels and consonants have one pronunciation, retaining that sound when placed in any combination of other letters/sounds.

As an American speaker of English, I find it odd to have such a limited palette of sounds, but I have found at least *this* part of learning Czech to be straightforward. (Many others are complicated.) For Czechs learning to speak English, on the other hand, the array of pronunciation possibilities and sound ambiguities in English is dizzying. I first noticed this problem when I introduced myself to my landlord's boyfriend, Jan "Honza" Škoda, when he offered to help me move into my Prague apartment in 2002.

Honza had seen my name on the lease document; working from the written form of it, he treated the *e* as Czechs typically do, similar to the short *e* that Americans would use in pronouncing "pet" or "leg," and pronounced it with an aspirated interruption in the middle of the "ee" sound. In standard practice, Czechs treat each vowel as an independently sounding element in a word. In saying the genitive plural of the word *studie* (studies) according to formal usage, Czechs reemphasize the second *i* at the end of the word: *studii*. Honza thus addressed me using an utterance that to me sounded like "layhay." Until we discussed the issue and I explained how to pronounce my name, I thought he was using a Czech word I had never heard. This sort of linguistic confusion has happened often as I continue to learn how to use the Czech language, and shows that the interface between Czech and English (especially as it is approached by Czechs as part of bluegrass music making) is often full of gaps and missed connections. The terminology and parlance of bluegrass music is difficult even for native English speakers. The Bluegrass Australia website used to include a list of "Commonly misspelled Bluegrass words" that clarified the spelling (and in some cases pronunciation) of a number of unusual names and items, for example, "Dobro," "chord (not cord)," "Jambalaya," and "McCoury [pronounced Mac-cure-ree]."[2]

Czechs often pride themselves on transcending this sort of adaptation and seek to distinguish themselves by using the "original American" pronunciation. The costumes a band will wear on stage at a concert (or the clothes that a fan might choose to wear to a bluegrass festival) can signal an affinity for a certain style of music, for instance, Stetson hats and string ties are one way for a band to announce to audiences that their musical approach is heavily influenced by Flatt and Scruggs (who often wore those items on stage); and a band's casual street clothes might signal that they don't feel constrained by traditional formal or stylistic boundaries. Likewise, the ways that common bluegrass-related words are articulated in speech can signal a desire to reflect knowledge of, allegiance to, or dislike of a certain community of language/music usage.

Naming

In Czech practice, individual people and institutions are often identified and reidentified through extensive traditions of renaming and nicknaming. One standard transformation is the diminutive (*zdrobnělina*), a convention that I, after a decade of use, am still unable to use fluently because—unlike Czech spelling—it is so idiosyncratic and rife with exceptions. These diminutives extend to the first and second degree, creating in the case of *strom*, "tree," the diminutives *stromek* and the even more diminuted *stromeček*. Diminution often increases with familiarity and affection; note that *stromeček*—the second-degree diminutive—is the Czech term for a Christmas tree, an important part of local holiday traditions. Indeed, the term seems almost exclusively used for the Christmas tree.

As with diminution, practices of nicknaming and name modification are as much ways to show affection as they are ways to establish new identities. There are standard alternative versions of names; for instance, men named Jan (John) are almost universally referred to as Honza. Still, these modifications involve much more fluidity than Czech grammatical structures. Czechs often use this area of linguistic flexibility to cross language boundaries through varieties of language play. As I explain in chapter 3, Zdeněk Roh's branding of his banjos with the "Roll's" name is one example. Petr Hrubý is a Czech bluegrasser whose rebranding of himself reveals the importance of language play to negotiations of identity boundaries. He has gone farther than many Czechs and established an alternative Anglophone persona, "Peter O. Ruby," that echoes his full Czech name, Petr Oldřich Hrubý. He uses this name in band announcements, on his websites, and in other official language.[3] Peter has spent considerable time in English-speaking countries (Australia and the United States), and his use of the alternate form of his name is a way for him to express his familiarity with English. Further, it matches his musical preferences: at the long-running Prague bluegrass jams that he has helped run since 2004, Peter tries to enforce (with varied success depending on the audience) an "English-only" singing policy.[4]

Czechs usually receive a nickname in the context of a community. When they take part in the translocal community of bluegrass (as they frequently do when engaging the international business world), they are often projecting themselves into an English-speaking community on Czech terms—or with Czech pronunciation. Petr Hrubý's more everyday Czech nickname is "Sam," a three-letter word with all kinds of complications. While his nickname is a reference to the English name Sam, it is usually pronounced with the typical Czech pronunciation, a broad *a* as in the American pronunciation of "father." This pronunciation reduces the connection to Americanness or the English language and allows the nickname to fit more easily into the spoken patterns of Czech grammatical transformations. With the broader *a* sound, it is easier for me to inflect "Sam" with cases like the vocative *Same* (Hey, Sam!) and the dative *Samovi* (to Sam). In addition, *sam* is already a word in Czech, an adverb meaning "alone." The Americanness of "Sam" is thus ambiguous, as Czech usage obscures its origin as an American-derived nickname. I would argue that Sam's nickname emerged as the one used by his community because it works well in both social and linguistic terms.

I rarely use nicknames in this text unless they are relevant to the discussion at hand, but I do use the standard familiar forms of given names—for instance, Honza instead of Jan. Likewise, I avoid the academic convention of using last names when referring to some of my Czech field colleagues. My choice of names for them in this book indicates the degree to which I am aware of each person's background and the depth of the relationship we share—the informal discourse in which our relationships (and this entire book project) are rooted. I use first names to refer to people with whom I am more comfortable, and I use last names when I do not draw on a deep relationship in quoting and explaining what they say and/or write.

This system is an approximation of the forms of address that are possible in the Czech language. As I have learned through awkward experiences of misuse, the formal and informal forms of "you" (*vy* and *ty*, respectively) are strictly adhered to in Czech usage, both informal and formal. Even in the contrived conversation of a structured interview, Czechs I spoke with would often halt our discourses to clarify what mode of address we would use. Most often, they would ask that I use the informal *ty* to address them. In an attempt to provide some sense of the texture of the discourse that led to the understandings in this project, in my writing

I simply use the name that I would use to talk to and about these colleagues in normal conversation.

A more prosaic difference between Czech and American usage is the treatment of proper nouns that are not personal names—specifically the capitalization of initial letters when a proper noun such as a title or the name of a place or organization consists of multiple words. I have most often used the Czech convention in this text, which is to capitalize only the first word of a title or non-personal name, as well as any other proper nouns within it. With some Czech compound proper nouns, however, I have used the American convention of starting all major parts of speech with initial capital letters, since the terms are often used in American environments. For example, I have chosen to use the American convention for the band Druhá Tráva, who often tour in the United States, even though *tráva* is a common noun meaning "grass." In a Czech context, however—in a news article, for example—the band's name may be rendered, following the Czech convention, as Druhá tráva.

Some Czech words are used in foreign contexts without the diacritics that are important for Czech pronunciation. For example, the name of a scholar whose work I cite in this text works in England and is listed on his university web page as Petr Jehlička, but he is also identified on some of the articles in his list of publications as Petr Jehlicka[5]—a reminder that Czechness does not always fit into the frames of global discourse, and that Czechs often have to adapt to make their voices heard outside of their own territory.

Amerika, Americanism, and Americanists

There are a variety of terms that I could use to categorize my colleagues' engagement with Americanness. First and foremost is the word *Amerika*, which is a commonly used term for the United States. The country's official name in Czech is Spojené státy americké, a formal translation that is seldom used. Czechs often refer to "the States" or to "America" (the latter of which they write with the *k*).

Most often I have chosen to use the word "Americanist" to describe projects like bluegrass music making or Indianism that provide a physical or audible form for this imagined "Amerika." As both an adjective and a designation for individual music makers and projects, this term includes a sense of the mediation of "America" that I perceive in these Czech efforts. While the field of American studies and other scholarly disciplines are populated by more official "Americanists," I have chosen the term to describe my Czech colleagues as a way of recognizing the legitimacy of their efforts, which in many cases are as well researched and thorough as scholarly Americanist work.

In a discussion about this project, Michelle Kisliuk proposed "Americanish" as a term that would highlight the quasi-Americanness of Czech bluegrass and other "America"-based projects. While I appreciate the humor in the formulation, feeling that this sort of wordplay would fit with the sensibilities of Czech bluegrassers, it does not always reflect the seriousness of the work or the play involved. Another usage of "Americanist" has a relevant political meaning, indicating support for the

United States and its policies; it is often used to describe intense patriotism or even chauvinism. This sense of the term can sometimes apply to Czech Americanists, who—like so many of us—often follow affect rather than reason in pursuit of their passions.

I include another possible term: "Americana" is often used to differentiate commercial activity from more academic "Americanist" projects, or to simply refer to the objects of American material culture. This category usually includes the kind of patriotic and nostalgic kitsch that adorns the walls of some "family-style" restaurants, "Main Street USA" displays in theme parks and model railroads, and other sites for idealization of "America." The word has also been adopted by some Americanist scholars as a label for the study of "American popular culture," but retains its connections to material culture and circulation through commerce.[6]

"Americana" also gained currency in musical circles after the release in 2000 of the film *O Brother, Where Art Thou?* "Americana" serves as an overarching designation for the country and folk music of the sort featured in that film, its soundtrack, and related productions. The *-ana* suffix refers to a distance between audiences and an authenticated cultural icon or situation. The commercial overtones of the term are underlined by the fact that the Americana Music Association was founded in 1999, when bluegrass, old-time, blues, gospel, and related genres were gaining ground in the US popular music business. To me, this term most clearly refers to entrepreneurial imagination and commercial intent.

I, like my bluegrass colleagues, am an Americanist. While this study is based in music and in social interactions, it is also about "America." To make this focus clear, I have drawn from the naming conventions and outlook of fields like "Africana studies" to propose "Americana studies" as a term to nuance the variety of American studies that pays attentions to Americanist projects like those detailed in this volume. As a way of addressing socioaesthetic practices, materials, and phenomena associated with America, particularly with the United States, Americana studies could allow a wider discussion of the importance of "America" on a global scale, and how elements of Americanness are constructed and performed outside of the US.

NOTES

Introduction

1. A recording of this performance is available from the State Library and Archives of Florida: "Saturday Performances at the 1991 Florida Folk Festival (Folklife Area/ Stage III) (Tape 3)," https://www.floridamemory.com/items/show/240540.

Chapter 1. Place, Meaning, Community, and In-Betweenness

1. My translation, made with aid from Zbyněk Bureš, who corrected my transcription and translation. All translations that follow are also mine except where noted. Of course, I bear all responsibility for errors in translation—please contact me if you see anything that isn't correct.

2. *Quartet* (Duna Records, 1993). Czech lyrics from http://petrkus.unas.cz/stranka.html, accessed October 9, 2007.

3. "Bluegrasser" (in Czech, *bluegrassák*) is a commonly used insider term for participants who enliven the music in any number of ways; the lines among players, listeners, and other participants (fans, business owners, etc.) are often blurred in both US and Czech usage. This word blends well with Christopher Small's (1998) holistic concept of music making or "musicking" as outlined in his book by that title.

4. There are a growing number of studies of country music activity outside the United States. One of the first scholarly books about bluegrass was by Japanese popular music scholar Toru Mitsui (1967). In addition to Dent (2009), the scholarship that I have consulted is mostly by ethnomusicologists, including Solli's (2006) work on Norwegian country music and Goertzen's (1988) article on the inroads

of American recordings and the growth of local country performance in Vienna. In constructing my framework for considering Czech Americanism, I have also looked more broadly, to Americanist Mel van Elteren (1996), who provides insight as to why country music hasn't flourished in the Netherlands, and to work by Helt (1977), who identifies a "boom" in German country music. Elsewhere (Bidgood 2010) I review Graeme Smith's (2005) volume on Australian country music.

5. Dick Hebdige's (1979) work on subcultures formed a foundation for later ideas, including Will Straw's (1991) work on popular music scenes. Bennett (2004) provides an excellent summary of scholarship on music scenes since Straw. Lee and Peterson (2004) provide a case study of an online "virtual" country music scene that informs the discussions of transcription and other forms of learning that I present in chapter 4 and the issues of fidelity that I discuss in chapter 5.

6. There are several active state and regional bluegrass associations in the United States (California's is one of the most significant); the two largest national groups are the International Bluegrass Music Association (IBMA) and the Society for the Preservation of Blue Grass Music of America (SPBGMA).

7. In using "paranoid," I follow Eve Sedgwick (2003, 124), who uses this term in critiquing practices of criticism that, in the years since Paul Ricoeur articulated a "hermeneutics of suspicion," "may have made it less rather than more possible to unpack the local, contingent relations between any given piece of knowledge and its narrative/epistemological entailments for the seeker, knower, or teller." I prefer what Sedgwick calls "reparative" readings, in which one strives to find ways to find the good, to connect constructively instead of deconstructing.

8. Adorno's (2002, 446) critiques of pop music hinge on mass consumption of pseudo-individualized products. De Certeau (De Certeau and Rendall 1988), Crafts, Cavicchi, and Keil (1993), and Frith (1992) offer a reparative reading of this consumption.

9. "Small" according to Wallis and Malm's definition (1984).

10. Reasonably priced for me, that is—the monthly rent of 10,000 Czech crowns was most of a local teacher's monthly salary. The roughly $350 monthly cost was well within my Fulbright-supported budget, however.

11. Fulbright Journal no. 1, 123–124.

12. There are other examples of this model for music and social relations in postsocialist cultures. See Urban and Evdokimov (2004) for an overview of Russian *kollektiv* community formation around American blues music, and Howard (2003) for a sociological study of civil society and postsocialism.

13. Interview with Ondřej Holoubek, February 29, 2008.

14. Interviews with Petr Hejkal, August 12, 2009; Rostislav Fischer, June 16, 2008; and Marko Čermák, May 3, 2008.

Chapter 2. Czech Bluegrass Histories and Backgrounds

1. Bluegrassová asociace České republiky (the Bluegrass Association of the Czech Republic) was founded in 1995. See http://www.bacr.cz/, accessed April 2, 2017.

2. These last three are Czech bluegrass instrument makers. See chapter 5 for more details and discussion. Gibson and Martin are US producers of iconic instruments within bluegrass communities.

3. Bidgood, Journal, October 12, 2007.

4. Note Čvančara's use of English for the piece of music, which in Czech is "Má vlast": "Napsal přeci 'My Country' a do své opery *Prodaná nevěsta* umístil Indiána. To je další důkaz, že tohle všecko začalo už v roce 1860." See also Bolz (1999), Kalshoven (2006), and Peprník (2008), who discuss Czech and German use of native American identities and lore in a variety of contexts.

5. Roach (1996, 46–47) offers an evocative reading of the exoticization of "America" performed in Purcell's *Dido and Aeneas*, considering this phenomenon as an early projection of the "Black Atlantic."

6. May's writings, which are widely available in both German and English, also include tales of adventures in the Middle East and elsewhere. *Winnetou* (2006) is a good example of his "Old West" stories.

7. I will discuss this project's parallel situation (the relevance of Czech bluegrass-related activity to American bluegrassers and vice versa) in chapter 5.

8. Or perhaps more specifically London's stories that romanticize frontier life and adventure, such as *White Fang* and *Call of the Wild*.

9. See Williams (2007) on *Wandervögel* and the "youth movement" in Germany in the late Wilhelmine period, especially chapter 3, "The Roots of Organized Youth Hiking: *Wandervögel*, Youth Cultivators, and Moral Panic, 1900–1915," 107–146. The YMCA has largely phased out its "Indian Guides" program; the National Longhouse organization is an offshoot that continues to appropriate native American imagery and practices in the name of (nonnative) recreation. See http://www.nationallonghouse.org/, accessed March 25, 2017.

10. *Sokol* means "falcon." See Dimond (2007) for an explanation of nationalism and the Czech Sokols in the early twentieth century.

11. See, for example, http://cs.wikipedia.org/wiki/Tramping. (I cite Wikipedia here not as a source for my own personal knowledge, but as a manifestation of this account, which I have heard in informal conversation.)

12. *Přírodou a životem k čistému lidství: Příručka českých junák* (Prague: Dědictví Komenského, 1920).

13. For more on this subject, see the second chapter of Reidinger's dissertation (2007, 68–127), entitled "'Tramping,' or How History Was Made for the Working Class, and How Bourgeois Marxists Made Out Like Bandits in Real Estate."

14. See http://www.slapeto.cz/ and http://www.slapetorevivalband.cz/, accessed December 12, 2010.

15. The collection *Americká lidová poezie* (American folk poetry) (Dorůžka 1961) was an influential resource for 1960s musical Americanists, who worked from the texts and melodies in this volume. The book's title emphasized the "folkness" of the American materials it contained, even as their foreignness and "folk" label made them modern and cosmopolitan.

16. Čermák tells this story in an interview segment in *Banjo Romantika*. This radio show and the banjo theme that opened it are documented in a US government documentary film, *The Story of American Forces Network (AFN)* (1962), a thirty-minute piece (the segment on the *Stickbuddy Jamboree* show starts at around 24:00) that is accessible online, including at https://archive.org/details/gov.archives.arc.2569813, accessed March 25, 2017.

17. Čermák uses the Czech figure of speech *u nás*, which literally means "near us" and is used figuratively to mean "at our place" (like the French *chez nous*), and by extension to refer to something happening or located within the Czech Republic.

18. This recording was made available thanks to the efforts of Gene Deitch, an American expatriate living in Prague since the late 1950s, and a friend of Seeger. Deitch used his original tapes from the concert (which were also used, he attests, for a recording on the Czech Supraphon label).

19. Interview with Marko Čermák, May 3, 2008.

20. Čermák used the nickname (Fučíkárna) for what is now known as the Výstaviště Praha-Holešovice (exhibition grounds in the Holešovice borough north of the center of Prague), and which was known before 1989 as the Park kultury a oddechu Julia Fučíka (the Julius Fučík Park of Culture and Relaxation).

21. Čermák had originally used the thumb and three fingers to play; the Scruggs style, or "three-finger style," uses the thumb and two other fingers.

22. I have provided the English translation for Kamarádí taborových ohně; the other groups used both their Czech and English band names according to circumstance—this flexibility was a necessary part of working as an Americanist musician in this period.

23. For an overview of post-1945 rock-oriented popular music history in the Czech lands, see Elavsky (2005, 101–172). Josef Kotek's (1998) history is one of the few Czech-language monographs covering postwar pop music, and provides a wealth of historical detail that complements Elavsky's work.

24. See Austin (2000) for a thorough explanation and archeology of a variety of categories of language acts.

25. Deleuze and Guattari (2002, 10) reinterpret the relationship of an insect and a flower, stating that as a wasp feeds and transports pollen from an orchid, "the wasp is . . . deterritorialized, becoming a piece in the orchid's reproductive apparatus. But it reterritorializes the orchid by transporting its pollen." For Yurchak (2006, 115), this sort of relation is a "veritable becoming, a becoming-wasp of the orchid and a becoming-orchid of the wasp," in which one system is deterritorialized while the other is reterritorialized, and vice versa.

26. I used three versions of the song lyrics to create this translation. The first is from a band's compilation of performing repertoire; the other two are lyric collections by music fans. See http://hpsk.sweb.cz/frame_main.html; http://vlcakuv-zpevnik.websnadno.cz/Pisne-ohnu-a-country.html; http://www.velkyzpevnik.cz/zpevnik/taborova-klasika/bluegrass, all accessed August 15, 2015.

27. In an interview I conducted with him on May 22, 2016, Lubor Hejda, bassist for the Brno-based band NaEx during the early 1990s, claimed that he wrote it.

Chapter 3. Making Bluegrass at Home, Abroad, and In Between

1. Kristin Solli's (2006) study of country music in Norway includes a discussion of alcohol-consumption practices linked to festivals and other special occasions (115–117).

2. https://www.youtube.com/watch?v=5Z7jZj8qI_o, accessed June 5, 2015.

3. In the fall of 2009, I visited a factory near Prague where CNC (computer numerical control) routers are programmed to carry out the rough shaping of wooden parts for viola da gambas and cellos. As of 2017, both Jaroslav Průcha and Zdeněk Roh are using this technology in building their instruments.

4. Linn (1994) adds credence to the claim, made in the title of Gura and Bollman's (1999) volume on the instrument in the nineteenth century, that the banjo is indeed "America's Instrument."

5. This bit of stage talk begins the first track of the *Pete Seeger in Prague* CD, which is labeled "T for Texas."

6. Michael Cronin (2003) deftly weaves this old definition into his discussion of globalization.

Chapter 4. Learning and Playing Americanness on the Fiddle

1. Bidgood fieldnotes, August 16, 2007.

2. While Titon (2001) finds in the early twentieth-century recordings of "old-time" fiddlers' performances a simple explanation for the fascination with "old-time" music that would continue for the rest of the century, Gavin Campbell (2004) and David Whisnant (1983) find more sinister motives behind the recourse to tradition in the early 1900s. The performance of racial consciousness in fiddling has a long history in the Americas, stretching back to the early colonial days. I will discuss this issue in more detail as it pertains to bluegrass and fiddling in the Czech Republic toward the end of this chapter.

3. I use the term "antimodern" in the sense in which Lears (1994, xv) employs it, to indicate the ambivalence and affinity for the modern, and modern American society's "complex blend of accommodation and protest" with regard to modernity.

4. http://www.youtube.com/watch?v=ssVborBaUNw&feature=related, accessed February 18, 2017.

5. Čermák received the IBMA Distinguished Achievement Award in 2007 for his role in popularizing the five-string banjo in Central Europe. See https://ibma.org/awards/recipient-history#distinguished, accessed February 18, 2017.

6. I discuss the band's experiences in Germany more in chapter 5, in the section on Czechs' regional and global influence in the bluegrass world.

7. Interview with Franta Kacafirek, June 3, 2008.

8. The mandolin's role in the standard bluegrass instrumental ensemble is to provide an off-beat rhythmic strum that alternates with the bass's clear playing of on-beat pulses. As a mandolin player, I have therefore spent countless hours developing a feel for the off-beat, and a taste for that part of the metric structure.

9. Jirka's ideas here are a good example of the model of "escape" proposed by Reidinger (2007) as one of the motivations for Americanist play.

10. Interview with Jirka Králík, September 21, 2007.

11. Ibid.

12. Interview with Slávka Franclíková, February 6, 2008. I use a simple ethnopoetic formatting here and for interview and other speech material that follows, to emphasize the spoken nature of what my Czech colleagues said and convey *how* they said it. I have inserted a line break for any pause that breaks the thread of speech, used my judgment to add implied words or phrases in brackets, and used ellipsis points to indicate where I cut out irrelevant material.

13. Ibid.

14. I have kept up with Slávka via social media, learning of her move in 2013, her experiences playing bluegrass with groups in New Zealand, and then her move back to the Czech Republic in 2015.

15. Ibid.

16. Ibid.

17. Ibid.

18. http://www.namodro.net/, accessed August 13, 2010.

19. Interview with Slávka Franclíková, February 6, 2008.

20. Verbs in the Czech language take two forms to indicate aspect. Perfective forms indicate one-time completed actions, while imperfective forms describe repeated or continuing actions.

21. Interview with Slávka Franclíková, February 6, 2008.

22. Ibid.

23. Ibid.

24. In a recent volume on "gender, race, and rusticity in country music," Pamela Fox (2009) expands on Peterson's work, focusing on the development of the carefully marked roles of early country music, and how they persist in contemporary forms.

25. Interview with Slávka Franclíková, February 6, 2008.

26. *Podzimní bluegrassová dílna*, self-produced video recording made by the workshop's organizer, Jindřich Hylmar, and distributed to workshop participants on DVD in 2007.

27. In the early twentieth century, academic attention to Roma was rare; see Hübschmannová (2007) for more on the history of Romistics (the study of the Roma language and people) in the Czech lands. There is now a unit for *Romistika* within the Department of Central European Studies at Charles University; see http://www.romistika.eu/.

28. Geoff Mann (2008) is one of many scholars who have recently discussed ways in which the production of whiteness in country music can be considered as part of the production of American culture and the sorts of "Americana" that Czechs consume and reproduce. Allen Farmelo (2001) proposes steps toward establishing "alternative" narratives about bluegrass that are more inclusive of African Americans.

29. Rosenberg's (2005, 272–300) description of bluegrass festivals in the 1960s and 1970s includes many references to the "ecumenical" aspects of the events,

and how a diversity of social classes and regionally identified people communed around the music. The racial diversity, however, was far less extensive than that of class and region.

30. http://www.martinzak.cz/en/martin.htm, accessed September 28, 2010.

31. There are many exceptions to this generalization. Early string band recordings feature all sorts of banjo playing: two- and three-finger styles, as well as a variety of frailing and clawhammer approaches. While many old-time players play clawhammer or other down-stroke styles exclusively, there are exceptions: the Foghorn Stringband has used a three-finger banjo style in their recordings, for example.

32. Interview with Jan Čermák, August 12, 2009.

33. Ibid.

34. A recent recording by Martin Žák challenges this idea, featuring a reperformance of a nineteenth-century minstrel show skit based on the fiddle tune "The Arkansas Traveler." Martin Žák and Věra Štaiglová, *Šlágry ze staré almary: 14 old-time country písniček* (Country Home CH CD902, compact disc, 2007).

35. Interview with Jan Čermák, August 12, 2009.

36. Interview with Rakovnickej Potok members, August 12, 2009.

Chapter 5. Singing Truth, Fidelity, and Play in Czech Bluegrass Gospel

1. "Balbín's poetic little pub," an institution in Prague's folk and independent music scene.

2. Translated with assistance from Zbyněk Bureš. Concert performance, November 13, 2007, author's field recordings (.mpg file). A video recording of the whole song is accessible online at http://www.youtube.com/watch?v=uv8m-OMckgI, accessed February 18, 2017.

3. Quicksilver is a well-regarded US gospel bluegrass group, the source for many of Reliéf's songs and arrangements. The piece Tomáš refers to, "Since Jesus Came into My Heart," is on the same album as "There Is a God": Doyle Lawson and Quicksilver, *There's a Light Guiding Me* (Sugar Hill 3845, compact disc, 1996).

4. Interview with Tomáš Dvořák, April 3, 2008. On this occasion Tomas spoke with me for more than an hour in English. His vocabulary is extensive, but at times limited in detail, which gives his ideas a simplistic, forceful edge that I suspect he only sometimes intended.

5. Appearance was crucial to Monroe. Cleo Davis, the first "Blue Grass Boy," recalls that when there was no money coming in from the band's performances in the early lean years, Monroe wouldn't pay him a salary but did cover the costs of his laundry and haircuts (Rosenberg 2005, 45).

6. See the unnumbered photo sections in Rosenberg (2005) and Smith (2000).

7. At least two of those "boys" were women. See http://doodah.net/bgb, accessed February 18, 2017, for an exhaustive database that details the changing lineup of the Blue Grass Boys.

8. https://ibma.org/awards/recipient-history#gospel; http://www.nytimes.com/ref/arts/music/08grammy-list.html, both accessed March 26, 2017.

9. See Bernhardt's (2001) anthropological account of contemporary bluegrass gospel performers for more examples and analysis.

10. Steve Martin, "Atheists Don't Have No Songs," on Steve Martin and the Steep Canyon Rangers, *Rare Bird Alert* (Rounder Records, 2011).

11. This self-released disc, *Old Dreams and New Dreams*, is not commercially available; the song I wrote is entitled "Where I Belong" and includes common gospel-song images of lost sheep, shepherds, and prodigal sons reaching a (heavenly) home.

12. The song is titled "Lodní zvon zvoní" and has been retexted to tell the story of a drunken sailor's departure for a long journey. Released on the vinyl LP *Greenhorns '71* (Panton, 1971).

13. Interview with Zbyněk Bureš, May 4, 2008.

14. Interview with Zbyněk Bureš, June 3, 2008.

15. Interview with Tomáš Dvořák, April 3, 2008.

16. Interview with Ondra Holoubek, February 29, 2008.

17. Interview with Tomáš Dvořák, April 3, 2008.

18. Ibid.

19. In foregrounding my experience here, I am responding to ethnomusicologist Melvin Butler's (2007, 114) call for transparent and reflexive discussion of "religious subjectivities" in music-faith ethnographic writing. At the same time, though, I am cautious about the way I am using this subjectivity—unlike Titon, I am not proposing that musical experience trumps what anthropologist Glenn Hinson (2000, 330) calls "supernatural experience." Hinson critiques statements such as that which I excerpt from Titon, statements that imply a relativist conception of religious experiences being "real *for them*" (emphasis in the original).

20. Interview with Tomáš Dvořák, April 3, 2008.

21. Elsewhere (Bidgood 2015) I discuss the importance of "play" in Czech bluegrass in more depth, drawing more intensively on Drewal's (1992) ideas of ethnography as a playful, improvisatory response to the emergent performance of life and fieldwork and Huizinga's (1955) conceptions of the boundaries and rules of play.

A Tag: America/*Amerika*

1. Ralph was a featured guest artist on Petr Kůs's record *Nezralé mládí* (Good Day Records, 2006). See Fámy's website, http://www.famy.cz/#HISTORIE, accessed March 29, 2017.

2. The extent of interest in these stories is indicated by the fact that there is an English-language Wikipedia entry on them: https://en.wikipedia.org/wiki/Rychlé_šípy, accessed August 31, 2016.

3. Interview with Marko Čermák, June 10, 2008.

4. After ceasing to perform in the early 2010s, the members of Reliéf regrouped to take part in a 2015 video production documenting the Czech bluegrass scene, but as of this writing they are no longer working together as a band.

5. See https://www.deeringbanjos.com/collections/deering-tony-trischka-model-banjos, accessed February 18, 2017.

6. http://www.bobes-banjo.cz/index.html, accessed March 29, 2017.

7. As of this writing, the Hot Diggity Bluegrass Band (based in Auckland, New Zealand) still uses photos that include Slávka, taken when she was a member of the group. See one of their social media sites here: https://www.youtube.com/channel/UCwxeeMoBQktc6iJSrMlr2vg, accessed March 29, 2017.

8. Interview segments from *Banjo Romantika* (2015).

9. Interview with Marko Čermák, June 10, 2008.

10. In checking over my translation of this conversation, bluegrasser Zbyněk Bureš wasn't sure how to best translate the verb *zachovat*, which can mean to preserve, prevent, or keep. Drawing on the body of English that he knows best (bluegrass and country repertory), Zbyněk recalled the 1950s Stanley Brothers lyric "Keep a memory of our love, dear" and suggested that "keep" would be the best translation.

Notes on Language

1. I have heard both lay and expert observers make this case. I first heard it from Laura Janda, who in 2001–2002 was my professor of Czech at the University of North Carolina at Chapel Hill, and an authority in the field of Slavic languages.

2. The list is no longer there, but it was at http://www.bluegrass.org.au/index.cfm?pid=111342 when I last accessed it on October 27, 2010.

3. This persona is part of a musical project and a performance persona. Petr called his band "Peter O. Ruby with All Bells and Whistles," a large mouthful for most Czech speakers, who often refer to them as "Bells a Whistles." You can see them in a live performance from 2006 at https://www.youtube.com/watch?v=k-4emBETPwE, accessed March 29, 2017.

4. Hrubý has administered a website for the jam that includes a statement that "English is standard"; see http://folkjam.org/recurring-jam/cz/pr/prague/open-bluegrass-jam-session-prague-restaurace-u-růženy, accessed April 1, 2017.

5. See http://open.academia.edu/PetrJehlicka and http://www.open.ac.uk/research/main/people/pj586-0, both accessed April 2, 2017.

6. See, for example, *Americana: The Journal of American Popular Culture, 1900 to Present*, http://www.americanpopularculture.com/journal/index.htm, accessed November 8, 2010

GLOSSARY OF CZECH TERMS

bendžo: banjo. While many Czechs use the English word without modification, some prefer the transliterated form, which reveals a Czech tendency to heighten and narrow American vowels.

český: Czech..

chajda: cabin. Marko Čermák uses this term to describe his cabin, "El Toro." A cabin made with round logs is often called a *roubenka*. (Note that in Czech, the consonant *ch* forms a single unit that appears in the alphabet between *h* and *i*. Because most of the readers of this book will likely not know Czech, however, it seemed more helpful to list the *ch*- words here along with the *c*- words.)

chalupa: A cottage not purpose-built for recreation; often an older village house adapted for recreational use. For example, Zdeněk Roh called the cottage where we stayed during the summer of 2007 in the town of Kašperské Hory a *chalupa*.

chata: cottage. A purpose-built recreational dwelling, usually built outside of cities, in a desirable and naturally appealing site, such as in the mountains or along a stream or lake.

Czechia: the English-language equivalent of Česko, the official short name for the Czech Republic. The Czechia Civic Initiative (http://www.go-czechia.com/) provides a comprehensive rationale for the use of this new name by Czechs themselves, outlining its social, political, and economic advantages. As of January 2017, I noticed that the Google company's maps service lists the country using the new term.

dílna: workshop. Used in the meaning of either an instrument-building workshop (such as the one where Zdeněk Roh builds banjos) or a weekend workshop where students learn about playing and singing bluegrass.

kroj: Czech folkloric costume, usually ornately handcrafted, and originating from a certain locality.
kulturní dům: house of culture. Municipal cultural centers are frequently used as venues for bluegrass-related concerts and workshops.
old-timeový: old-time. The adjectival suffix *-ový* (the masculine form; the feminine is *-ová*, and neuter is *-ové*) is often added to foreign words.
osada: camp. Tramp camps were established as bases for tramping activity, and have become sites for Americanist accessorizing. Many sport evocative names, such as Dakota, Harvard, and Stará Hiawata ("Old Hiawatha").
pension (or *penzion*): a category of accommodation rated below that of a hotel.
seberealizace: self-realization. A goal for individuals during Czechoslovak normalization; often carried out in opposition to official policies. Some forms of Americanism seem to have been accepted as allowable forms of self-realization.
skaut: scout. Scouting grew among Czechs during the early 1900s as part of the popular international movement led by Lord Baden-Powell and other organizers. Many historians assert that Czech tramping developed from "wild scouts" who liked the woodcraft elements of the practice but not the regimentation.
stáhnout/stahovat: to transcribe or download. The perfective and imperfective forms of this verb are used to refer to downloading from the internet and transcribing recorded music into a written form.
strejda (informal version of *strýc*): uncle. This term is also used to express a sense of kinship with a male person (the female equivalent for "auntie" is *téta*). I was known as "strejda Lee" by the children of some of my Czech bluegrass colleagues.
trampské písničky: tramp songs. Many of the songs that date from the early period of tramping in the 1920s are still sung today around tramp campfires and at "potlatch" ceremonies, such as "Cariboo" by Jarka Mottl and "Vlajka" by Jan Korda.
transkribovat: to transcribe.
vážná hudba: classical music/art music. Literally, "serious music."
věřící: a (Christian) believer.
vono: it. The *v-* prefix adds emphasis. This term is not limited to talk about music, but is often used by bluegrassers to identify what they value in a musical experience.
vytvořit: to create or form.

REFERENCES

Adorno, Theodor W. 2002. "On Popular Music." In *Essays on Music: Theodor W. Adorno*, edited by Richard Leppert, 437–469. Berkeley: University of California Press.

Ash, Timothy Garton. 1990. *We, the People: The Revolution of '89 Witnessed in Warsaw, Budapest, Berlin and Prague*. New York: Cambridge University Press.

Austin, J. L. 2000. *How to Do Things with Words*. Cambridge, MA: Harvard University Press.

Averill, Gage. 2003. *Four Parts, No Waiting: A Social History of American Barbershop Harmony*. New York: Oxford University Press.

Bakhtin, M. M. 1990. *Art and Answerability: Early Philosophical Essays*. Edited by Michael Holquist and Vadim Liapunov. Austin: University of Texas Press.

———. 2004. *The Dialogic Imagination: Four Essays*. Edited by Michael Holquist. Austin: University of Texas Press.

Barany, Zoltan. 2002. *The East European Gypsies: Regime Change, Marginality, and Ethnopolitics*. New York: Cambridge University Press.

Bateson, Gregory. 1955. "A Theory of Play and Fantasy: A Report on Theoretical Aspects of the Project of Study of the Role of the Paradoxes of Abstraction in Communication." *Psychiatric Research Reports* 2: 39–51.

Bealle, John. "Self-Involvement in Musical Performance: Stage Talk and Interpretive Control at a Bluegrass Festival." *Ethnomusicology* 37, no. 1 (1993): 63–86.

Beckerman, Michael. 1996. "Kundera's Musical Joke and 'Folk' Music in Czechoslovakia, 1948–?" In *Retuning Culture: Musical Changes in Central and Eastern Europe*, edited by Mark Slobin, 37–53. Durham, NC: Duke University Press.

———. 2003. *New Worlds of Dvořák: Searching in America for the Composer's Inner Life*. New York: W. W. Norton and Co.

Bendix, Regina. 1997. *In Search of Authenticity: The Formation of Folklore Studies.* Madison: University of Wisconsin Press.

Bennett, Andy. 2004. "Consolidating the Music Scenes Perspective." *Poetics* 32, no. 3–4: 223–234.

Bennett, Andy, and Richard A. Peterson, eds. 2004. *Music Scenes: Local, Translocal and Virtual.* Nashville, TN: Vanderbilt University Press.

Bernhardt, Jack. 2001. "Performance, Faith, and Bluegrass Gospel: An Anthropological Journey with Jerry and Tammy Sullivan." In *Country Music Annual 2000*, edited by Charles K. Wolfe and James E. Akenson, 51–69. Lexington: University Press of Kentucky.

Bidgood, Lee. 2010. "Review of Graeme Smith, *Singing Australian: A History of Folk and Country Music.*" *Popular Music* 29: 312–313.

———. 2015. "Czech Bluegrass in Play." *Lidé Města / Urban People* 17, no. 2: 283–303.

———. Forthcoming. "The Americanist Imagination and Real Imaginary Place in Czech Bluegrass Songs." *Popular Music and Society.*

Black, Bob. 2005. *Come Hither to Go Yonder: Playing Bluegrass with Bill Monroe.* Urbana: University of Illinois Press.

Bolz, Peter. 1999. "Life among the 'Hunkpapas': A Case Study in German Indian Lore." In *Indians and Europe: An Interdisciplinary Collection of Essays*, edited by Christian F. Feest, 475–490. Lincoln: University of Nebraska Press.

Boym, Svetlana. 2001. *The Future of Nostalgia.* New York: Basic Books.

Bren, Paula. 2002. "Weekend Getaways: The Chata, the Tramp and the Politics of Private Life in Post-1968 Czechoslovakia." In *Socialist Spaces: Sites of Everyday Life in the Eastern Bloc*, edited by David Crowley and Susan E. Reid, 123–140. New York: Oxford University Press.

Brody, David. 1983. *The Fiddler's Fakebook.* New York: Oak Publications.

Buff, Margot. 2005. "Deep South Boheme." Accessed February 14, 2017. http://prague.tv/articles/art-and-culture/south-bohem.

Burawoy, Michael. 1999. "Afterword." In *Uncertain Transition: Ethnographies of Change in the Postsocialist World*, edited by Michael Burawoy and Katherine Verdery, 301–311. New York: Rowman and Littlefield.

Butler, Melvin. 2007. "Thoughts on the Intersection of Race and Faith in the Study of Popular Music." *Journal of Popular Music Studies* 19, no. 1: 113–117.

Campbell, Gavin James. 2004. *Music and the Making of a New South.* Chapel Hill: University of North Carolina Press.

Cantwell, Robert. 1984. *Bluegrass Breakdown: The Making of the Old Southern Sound.* Urbana: University of Illinois Press.

———. 1993. *Ethnomimesis: Folklife and the Representation of Culture.* Chapel Hill: University of North Carolina Press.

Carney, George O. 1974. "Bluegrass Grows All Around: The Spatial Dimensions of a Country Music Style." *Journal of Geography* 73, no. 4: 34–55.

———. 1998. "Western North Carolina: Culture Hearth of Bluegrass Music." In *Baseball, Barns, and Bluegrass: A Geography of American Folklife*, edited by George O. Carney, 286–321. Lanham, MD: Rowman and Littlefield.

Čermák, Marko. 1977. *Pětistrunné banjo* [Five-string banjo]. Prague: Supraphon.
———. 1998. *Banjo z mlžných lesů* [Banjo from the foggy woods]. Mnichovice: Country Home.
———. 2010. *Poslední romantik* [The last romantic]. Prague: Vaclάv Vávra.
Chari, Sharad, and Katherine Verdery. 2008. "Thinking between the Posts: Postcolonialism, Postsocialism, and Ethnography after the Cold War." *Comparative Studies in Society and History* 51, no. 1: 6–34.
Cherre, Vincent. 2013. "The Real Place of Appalachia in Bluegrass Music." in *The International Country Music Journal*, edited by Don Cusic, 27–40. Nashville, TN: Brackish.
Clifford, James. 1986. "Introduction: Partial Truths." In *Writing Culture: The Poetics and Politics of Ethnography*, edited by James Clifford and George E. Marcus, 1–26. Berkeley: University of California Press.
Connerton, Paul. 1989. *How Societies Remember*. New York: Cambridge University Press.
Crafts, Susan D., Daniel Cavicchi, and Charles Keil. 1993. *My Music: Explorations of Music in Daily Life*. Middletown, CT: Wesleyan University Press.
Craig, R. Stephen. 1988. "American Forces Network in the Cold War: Military Broadcasting in Postwar Germany." *Journal of Broadcasting and Electronic Media* 32, no. 3: 307–323.
Creed, Gerald W. 1998. *Domesticating Revolution: From Socialist Reform to Ambivalent Transition in a Bulgarian Village*. University Park: Pennsylvania State University Press.
Cronin, Michael. 2003. *Translation and Globalization*. New York: Routledge.
Cummings, Richard H. 2009. *Cold War Radio: The Dangerous History of American Broadcasting in Europe, 1950–1989*. New York: McFarland and Co.
De Certeau, Michel, and Steven Rendall. 1988. *The Practice of Everyday Life*. Berkeley: University of California Press.
Deleuze, Gilles, and Félix Guattari. 2002. *A Thousand Plateaus: Capitalism and Schizophrenia*. London: Continuum. First published 1987.
DeNora, Tia. 2003. *After Adorno: Rethinking Music Sociology*. New York: Cambridge University Press.
Dent, Alexander S. 2009. *River of Tears: Country Music, Memory, and Modernity in Brazil*. Durham, NC: Duke University Press.
Dimond, Mark. 2007. "The Sokol and Czech Nationalism, 1918–1948." In *Czechoslovakia in a Nationalist and Fascist Europe, 1918–1948*, edited by Mark Cornwall and R. J. W. Evans, 185–205. New York: Oxford University Press.
Dorůžka, Lubomír, ed. 1961. *Americká lidová poezie* [American folk poetry]. Prague: Státní nakladatelství krásné literatury a umění.
Drewal, Margaret Thompson. 1992. *Yoruba Ritual: Performers, Play, Agency*. Bloomington: Indiana University Press.
Elavsky, Charles Michael. 2005. "Producing 'Local' Repertoire: Czech Identity, Pop Music, and the Global Music Industry." PhD diss., University of Illinois at Urbana-Champaign.

Farmelo, Allen. 2001. "Another History of Bluegrass: The Segregation of American Popular Music, 1820–1900." *Popular Music and Society* 25, no. 1: 179–204.

Feld, Steven. 1984. "Sound Structure as Social Structure." *Ethnomusicology* 28, no. 3: 383–409.

Felske, Lorry W., and Beverly Rasporich. 2004. *Challenging Frontiers: The Canadian West*. Calgary: University of Calgary Press.

Finch, Mark. 2016. "Bluegrass in and around Toronto: Urban Scenes, Regional Imaginaries, and Divergent Trajectories." PhD diss., Memorial University of Newfoundland.

Fox, Aaron. 2004. *Real Country: Music and Language in Working-Class Culture*. Durham, NC: Duke University Press.

Fox, Pamela. 2009. *Natural Acts: Gender, Race, and Rusticity in Country Music*. Ann Arbor: University of Michigan Press.

Frayling, Christopher. 2006. *Spaghetti Westerns: Cowboys and Europeans from Karl May to Sergio Leone*. New York: IB Tauris.

Frith, Simon. 1992. "The Cultural Study of Popular Music." In *Cultural Studies*, edited by Lawrence Grossberg, Cary Nelson, and Paula Treichler, 174–186. New York: Routledge.

Fronek, Josef. 1999. *English-Czech, Czech English Dictionary*. Voznice: Leda.

Gardner, Robert. 2004. "The Portable Community: Mobility and Modernization in Bluegrass Festival Life." *Symbolic Interaction* 27, no. 2: 155–178.

Geertz, Clifford. 2000. "Deep Play: Notes on the Balinese Cockfight." In *The Interpretation of Cultures*, 412–453. New York: Basic Books.

Gelbart, Matthew. 2007. *The Invention of "Folk Music" and "Art Music": Emerging Categories from Ossian to Wagner*. New York: Cambridge University Press.

Goertzen, Chris. 1988. "Popular Music Transfer and Transformation: The Case of American Country Music in Vienna." *Ethnomusicology* 32, no 1: 1–21.

Goff, James. 2002. *Close Harmony: A History of Southern Gospel*. Chapel Hill: University of North Carolina Press.

Goldsmith, Thomas, ed. 2004. *The Bluegrass Reader*. Urbana: University of Illinois Press.

Gruber, Ruth Ellen. 2009. "Beyond Virtually Jewish: New Authenticities and Real Imaginary Spaces in Europe." *Jewish Quarterly Review* 99, no. 4: 487–504.

Gura, Philip F., and James F. Bollman. 1999. *America's Instrument: The Banjo in the Nineteenth Century*. Chapel Hill: University of North Carolina Press.

Guy, Roger. 2007. *From Diversity to Unity: Southern and Appalachian Migrants to Uptown Chicago, 1950–1970*. Lanham, MD: Rowman and Littlefield.

Habermas, Jürgen. 1979. *Communication and the Evolution of Society*. Boston: Beacon Press.

Hambly, Scott. 1980. "San Francisco Bay Area Bluegrass and Bluegrass Musicians: A Study in Regional Characteristics." *JEMF Quarterly* 16, no. 59: 111–117.

Hardwig, Bill. 2001. "Cocks, Balls, Bats, and Banjos: Masculinity and Competition in the Bluegrass Music of Bill Monroe." *Southern Quarterly* 39, no. 4: 35–48.

Hartford, John. 1999. *Good Old Boys*. Rounder CD 0462, compact disc.
Haslam, Gerald W., with Alexandra Haslam Russell and Richard Chon. 1999. *Workin' Man Blues: Country Music in California*. Berkeley: University of California Press.
Havel, Václav. 1989. *Living in Truth: Twenty-Two Essays Published on the Occasion of the Award of the Erasmus Prize to Václav Havel*. Edited by Jan Vladislav. Paperback ed. Boston: Faber and Faber.
Hebdige, Dick. 1979. *Subculture: The Meaning of Style*. London: Routledge.
Heim, Michael. 1982. *Contemporary Czech*. Bloomington, IN: Slavica Publishers.
Helt, Richard C. 1977. "A German Bluegrass Festival: The 'Country-Boom' and Some Notes on the History of American Popular Music in West Germany." *Journal of Popular Culture* 10, no. 4: 821–832.
Hinson, Glenn. 2000. *Fire in My Bones: Transcendence and the Holy Spirit in African American Gospel*. Philadelphia: University of Pennsylvania Press.
Hofman, Ana. 2009. "Yugomania: Music and Nostalgic Practices on the Internet." In *Voices of the Weak: Music and Minorities*, edited by Zuzana Jurková and Lee Bidgood, 216–225. Prague: Slovo 21.
Holý, Ladislav. 1996. *The Little Czech and the Great Czech Nation: National Identity and the Post-Communist Transformation of Society*. New York: Cambridge University Press.
Hood, Mantle. 1960. "The Challenge of Bi-musicality." *Ethnomusicology* 4, no. 2: 55–59.
Howard, Marc Morjé. 2003. *The Weakness of Civil Society in Post-Communist Europe*. New York: Cambridge University Press.
Hübschmannová, Milena. 2007. "Musings on Romistics." In *Minority: Construct or Reality? On Reflection and Self-Realization of Minorities in History*, edited by Zuzana Jurková, Blanka Soukupová, Hedvika Novotná, and Peter Salner, 18–33. Bratislava: Zingprint.
Huizinga, Johan. 1955. *Homo Ludens: A Study of the Play-Element in Culture*. Boston: Beacon.
Hurikán, Bob. 1990. *Dějiny trampingu* [History of tramping]. Prague: Novinář.
Jehlicka, Petr. 2008. "Indians of Bohemia: The Spell of Woodcraft on Czech Society, 1912–2006." In *Sport-Ethnie-Nation: Zur Geshichte und Soziologie des Sports in Nationalitatenkonflikten und bei Minoritaten*, edited by Diethelm Blecking and Marek Waic, 112–130. Baltamannsweiler: Schneider Verlag Hohengehren.
Jehlicka, Petr, and Joe Smith. 2007. "Out of the Woods and into the Lab: Exploring the Strange Marriage of American Woodcraft and Soviet Ecology in Czech Environmentalism." *Environment and History* 13, no. 2: 187–210.
Jirásek, Pavel. 1999. "Český meziválečný tramping" [Czech interwar tramping]. *Živel* 15 (December): 56–60.
Johnston, Jesse A. 2008. "The Cimbál (Cimbalom) in Moravia: Cultural Organology and Interpretive Communities." PhD diss., University of Michigan.
Jurková, Zuzana. 2007. "Uncovering Layers of Memory: A Diachronic Approach to the Music of Central European Jews and Roma." In *Minority: Construct or*

Reality? On Reflection and Self-Realization of Minorities in History, edited by Zuzana Jurková, Blanka Soukupová, Hedvika Novotná, and Petr Salner, 110–115. Bratislava: Zingprint.

Kalshoven, Petra Tjitske. 2006. "Plays on 'the Indian': Representations of Knowledge and Authenticity in Indianist Mimetic Practice." PhD diss., McGill University.

Kingsbury, Henry. 2001. *Music, Talent, and Performance: A Conservatory Cultural System*. Philadelphia: Temple University Press.

Kisliuk, Michelle. 1988. "'A Special Kind of Courtesy': Action at a Bluegrass Festival Jam Session." *TDR* 32, no. 3: 141–155.

Kisliuk, Michelle, and Kelly Gross. 2004. "What's the 'It' That We Learn to Perform? Teaching Baaka Music and Dance." In *Performing Ethnomusicology: Teaching and Representation in World Music Ensembles*, edited by Ted Solís, 249–260. Berkeley: University of California Press.

Kotek, Josef. 1995. "Lidovka a trampská píseň meziválečného období" [Lidovka and tramp song of the interwar period]. *Hudebni věda* 32, no. 2: 158–181.

———. 1998. *Dějiny české populární hudby a zpěvu* [History of Czech popular music and singing]. Prague: Academia.

Kresin, Susan, et al. 2000. *Čeština hrou* [Czech for fun]. 2nd ed. New York: McGraw-Hill Primis.

Kuras, Benjamin. 1996. *Czechs and Balances: A Nation's Survival Kit*. New York: Baronet.

Lass, Andrew. 1989. "What Keeps the Czech Folk 'Alive'?" *Dialectical Anthropology* 14, no. 1: 7–19.

Lears, T. J. Jackson. 1994. *No Place of Grace: Antimodernism and the Transformation of American Culture, 1880–1920*. Chicago: University of Chicago Press.

Lee, Steve S., and Richard A. Peterson. 2004. "Internet-Based Virtual Music Scenes: The Case of P2 in Alt.Country Music." In *Music Scenes: Local, Trans-Local and Virtual*, edited by Andy Bennett and Richard A. Peterson, 187–204. Nashville, TN: Vanderbilt University Press.

Linn, Karen. 1994. *That Half-Barbaric Twang: The Banjo in American Popular Culture*. Urbana: University of Illinois Press.

Lodge, Martin. 2009. "Music Historiography in New Zealand." In *Music's Intellectual History*, edited by Zdravko Blažeković and Barbara Dobbs Mackenzie, 625–632. New York: RILM.

London, Jack. 1998. *The Call of the Wild, White Fang, and Other Stories*. New York: Oxford University Press.

———. 2007. *The Road*. Piscataway, NJ: Rutgers University Press. First published 1907.

Macek, Jiří. 2001. *Country zpěvník II*. Cheb: G+W.

Malone, Bill C. 2002. *Don't Get above Your Raisin': Country Music and the Southern Working Class*. Urbana: University of Illinois Press.

Malone, Bill C., and Jocelyn Neal. 2010. *Country Music, USA*. Austin: University of Texas Press.

Mann, Geoff. 2008. "Why Does Country Music Sound White? Race and the Voice of Nostalgia." *Ethnic and Racial Studies* 31, no. 1: 73–100.

Markl, Jaroslav. 1963. "Czech Bagpipe Music." *Journal of the International Folk Music Council* 15: 72–74.

Massey, Doreen. 1994. *Space, Place, and Gender*. Minneapolis: University of Minnesota Press.

———. 2005. *For Space*. Thousand Oaks, CA: Sage.

May, Karl. 2006. *Winnetou*. Translated by Michael Shaw. London: Continuum. Original German ed. 1892.

Mitchell, Donald. 2000. *Critical Geography, An Introduction*. Malden, MA: Blackwell.

Mitsui, Tōru. 1967. *Burūgurasu ongaku* [Bluegrass music]. Toyohashi, Japan: Traditional Song Society, Aichi University.

Murphy, Cliff. 2014. *Yankee Twang: Country and Western Music in New England*. Urbana: University of Illinois Press.

Negus, Keith. 1999. *Music Genres and Corporate Cultures*. New York: Routledge.

Opekar, Aleš. 1998. "Early Czech Rock'n'roll: Social Conditions and Four Sounds in Preserved Recordings." In *Popular Music: Intercultural Interpretations*, edited by Tōru Mitsui, 349–356. Kanazawa: Kanazawa University.

Pavličíková, Helena. 2000. "The History of Czech Modern Folk Music." *Musicologica Olomucensia* 19, no. 5: 113–122.

Peprník, Michal. 2008. "The Affinity with the North American Indian in Czech Literary Discourse on the Democratic Roots of Czech National Culture." *Journal of Transatlantic Studies* 6, no. 2: 148–157.

Peterson, Richard A. 1997. *Creating Country Music: Fabricating Authenticity*. Chicago: University of Chicago Press.

Reidinger, Melinda. 2007. "Islands of Bourgeois Self-Realization in a Sea of Changes: A Century of Czech Cottaging." PhD diss., University of Virginia.

Roach, Joseph. 1996. *Cities of the Dead: Circum-Atlantic Performance*. New York: Columbia University Press.

Rockwell, Joti. 2007. "Drive, Lonesomeness, and the Genre of Bluegrass Music." PhD diss., University of Chicago.

Rosenberg, Neil V. 2005. *Bluegrass: A History*. Revised ed. Urbana: University of Illinois Press.

Rosenberg, Neil V., and Charles K. Wolfe. 2007. *The Music of Bill Monroe*. Urbana: University of Illinois Press.

Sammons, Jeffrey L. 1998. *Ideology, Mimesis, Fantasy: Charles Sealsfield, Friedrich Gerstäcker, Karl May, and Other German Novelists of America*. Chapel Hill: University of North Carolina Press.

Samuels, David W. 2005. *Putting a Song on Top of It: Expression and Identity on the San Carlos Apache Reservation*. Tucson: University of Arizona Press.

Schechner, Richard. 1985. "Performers and Spectators Transported and Transformed." In *Between Theater and Anthropology*, 117–150. Philadelphia: University of Pennsylvania Press.

———. 1988. "Playing." *Play and Culture* 1, no. 13: 3–19.

Scruton, Roger. 1988. "Masaryk, Patočka and the Care of the Soul." In *On Masaryk: Texts in English and German*, edited by Josef Novák, 111–128. Amsterdam: Rodopi.

Sedgwick, Eve Kosofsky. 2003. *Touching Feeling: Affect, Pedagogy, Performativity.* Durham, NC: Duke University Press.

Seeger, Pete. 2001. *Pete Seeger in Prague, 1964*. Flyright, Fly CD 68 and 69, compact discs. Recorded March 27–28, 1964.

Seton, Ernest Thompson. 1912. *The Book of Woodcraft and Indian Lore.* Garden City, NY: Doubleday,.

Shank, Barry. 2002. "'That Wild Mercury Sound': Bob Dylan and the Illusion of American Culture." *boundary 2* 29, no. 1: 97–123.

Sklar, Deidre. 1994. "Can Bodylore Be Brought to Its Senses?" *Journal of American Folklore* 107, no. 423: 9–22.

Škrobáková, Eva. 2002. "Bluegrass." MA thesis, Masaryk University.

Škvorecký, Josef. 1979. *The Bass Saxophone*. Translated by Káča Poláčková-Henley. New York: Knopf.

Small, Christopher. 1998. *Musicking: The Meanings of Performing and Listening.* Middletown, CT: Wesleyan University Press.

Smith, Graeme. 2005. *Singing Australian: A History of Folk and Country Music.* North Melbourne: Pluto Press Australia.

Smith, Mayne. 1965. "An Introduction to Bluegrass." *Journal of American Folklore* 78: 245–256.

Smith, Richard D. 2000. *Can't You Hear Me Callin': The Life of Bill Monroe, Father of Bluegrass*. Boston: Little, Brown and Co.

Šolle, Zdeněk. 1990. "Vojtěch Náprstek and His Era: Bohemia, the United States, and the Transmission of Cultures." *East Central Europe* 17, no. 1: 1–30.

Solli, Kristin. 2006. "North of Nashville: Country Music, National Identity, and Class in Norway." PhD diss., University of Iowa.

Solzhenitsyn, Alexander. 2004. "Live Not by Lies." *Index on Censorship* 33, no. 2: 203–207.

Spencer, Jon M. 1994. *Theomusicology*. Durham, NC: Duke University Press.

Stafford, Tim. 1987. "Rock Me in the Cradle of Bluegrass: Bluegrass Music in the Tri-Cities Region of Upper East Tennessee." *Bluegrass Unlimited* 22, no. 4: 18–24.

Stanley, Ralph, with Eddie Dean. 2009. *Man of Constant Sorrow: My Life and Times.* New York: Gotham Books.

Štecha, Pavel. 2001. *U nás: 1968–1990 / In Our Country*. Prague: Jaroslav Barta Studio.

Straw, Will. 1991. "Systems of Articulation, Logics of Change: Communities and Scenes in Popular Music." *Cultural Studies* 5, no. 3: 368–388.

Sutton-Smith, Brian. 2006. "Play and Ambiguity." In *The Game Design Reader: A Rules of Play Anthology*, edited by Katie Salen and Eric Zimmerman, 296–313. Cambridge, MA: MIT Press.

Sweet, Stephen. 1996. "Bluegrass Music and Its Misguided Representation of Appalachia." *Popular Music and Society* 20, no. 3: 37–51.

Tillich, Paul. 1957. *Dynamics of Faith*. New York: Harper and Row.

Titon, Jeff Todd. 1995. "Bi-musicality as Metaphor." *Journal of American Folklore* 108, no. 429: 287–297.

———. 1997. "Knowing Fieldwork." In *Shadows in the Field: New Perspectives for Fieldwork in Ethnomusicology*, edited by Gregory Barz and Timothy J. Cooley, 87–100. New York: Oxford University Press.

———. 2001. *Old-Time Kentucky Fiddle Tunes*. Lexington: University Press of Kentucky.

Townsend, Charles E. 1990. *A Description of Spoken Prague Czech*. Columbus, OH: Slavica Publishers.

Troutman, John W. 2013. "Steelin' the Slide: Hawai'i and the Birth of the Blues Guitar," *Southern Cultures* 19, no. 1: 26–52.

Turino, Thomas. *Music as Social Life: The Politics of Participation*. Chicago: University of Chicago Press, 2008.

Turner, Victor. 1982. *From Ritual to Theatre: The Human Seriousness of Play*. New York: Performing Arts Journal Publications.

Urban, Michael E., and Andrei Evdokimov. 2004. *Russia Gets the Blues: Music, Culture, and Community in Unsettled Times*. Ithaca, NY: Cornell University Press.

Van Elteren, Mel. 1996. "Country Music in the Netherlands: Why Is It Still Marginal?" *Popular Music and Society* 20, no. 3: 53–93.

Vondrák, Jiří, and Fedor Skotal. 2004. *Legendy Folku & Country: Jediný téměř úplný příběh folku, trampské, a country písně u nás* [Legends of folk and country: The only almost complete story of our folk, tramp, and country songs]. Brno: Jota.

Wallis, Roger, and Krister Malm. 1984. *Big Sounds from Small Peoples: The Music Industry in Small Countries*. London: Constable and Co.

Weber, A. Dana. 2012. "Staged Indians: Native Americans in German Theatre and Karl-May-Festivals." In *Visual Representations of Native Americans: Transnational Contexts and Perspectives*, edited by Karsten Fitz, 163–177. Heidelberg: Universitätsverlag Winter.

Whisnant, David E. 1983. *All That Is Native and Fine: The Politics of Culture in an American Region*. Chapel Hill: University of North Carolina Press.

Williams, John Alexander. 2007. *Turning to Nature in Germany: Hiking, Nudism, and Conservation, 1900–1940*. Stanford, CA: Stanford University Press.

Yurchak, Alexei. 2000. "Privatize Your Name: Symbolic Work in a Post-Soviet Linguistic Market." *Journal of Sociolinguistics* 4, no. 3: 406–434.

Yurchak, A. 2006. *Everything Was Forever, Until It Was No More: The Last Soviet Generation*. Princeton, NJ: Princeton University Press.

RECOMMENDED MEDIA

Note: This is not an exhaustive discography of Czech bluegrass, but rather a listing of material relevant to the people, sounds, and stories in this volume. For a wider (and updated) list of bands, festivals, and concerts, see the websites listed at the end of this section.

Audio

Banjo Romantika Soundtrack. Produced by Lee Bidgood, 2016. Compact disc.

The material in this collection all relates to the documentary film *Banjo Romantika*; there are musical performances from the film and a field recording of a jam, as well as studio-produced tracks from musicians featured in the film, such as Reliéf, Zdeněk Roh, and Luboš Malina. In addition, there is material from the Banjo Romantika Band, a flexible group composed mainly of American musicians who contributed performances of Czech songs for the film. This group includes East Tennessee State University faculty Dan Boner, Brandon Green, Adam Steffey, and Colleen Trenwith.

Bobek, Pavel. *Veď mě dál, cesto má* (Take me home, country roads). Bonton 491054 2, 1998. Compact disc.

This collection, originally released on LP in 1975, includes the title track (a translation of the John Denver number "Take Me Home, Country Roads," which proved to be a hit with Czechs as well), along with retextings of songs by Kris Kristofferson, Don McLean, Roger Miller, and Billy Edd Wheeler, reflecting in its smooth musical aesthetic the pop-oriented approach that dominated Nashville-based country music in the early to mid-1970s.

Cash, Johnny. *Koncert v Praze (In Prague Live)*. Columbia 1113 3278 ZD, 2015. Vinyl LP, compact disc. Recorded April 11, 1978.

The Czech Supraphon company released this LP in 1983, using material recorded at Johnny Cash's concert in Prague in 1978. The 2015 re-release of the record on both vinyl and compact disc (as well as streaming and downloading platforms) reflects the resurgence of interest in vinyl as a format, but also the exoticism of Czechs' interest in country music: the package reproduces the explanatory notes (in Czech, with English translation) by Mirek Černý. This concert is also available in video form on YouTube in various versions; most include the Czech-language commentary by singer Pavel Bobek, who at one point remarks that Cash is a *živá legenda* (living legend). Cash's impact on Czech country music cannot be underestimated; for example, his version of "Orange Blossom Special" was the one used by the Greenhorns when they covered (and retexted) that song.

Čermák, Marko, and Greenhorns. *Banjo z mlžných lesů* (Banjo from the foggy woods). Bonton 491038 2, 1998. Compact disc.

This collection highlights Marko's work with the Greenhorns, and accompanies a book by the same title: part memoir, banjo tutorial, part songbook.

Cop. *His Master's Cop*. Vopava, 2002. Compact disc.

Cop (their name comes from the Czech word for "ponytail," not anything to do with police) are a longstanding institution nationwide, but they are especially popular near their Western Bohemian base in Plzeň. Led by guitarist and singer Miroslav "Míša" Leicht, they adopt a mode of biker-influenced costume (including black leather, big belt buckles, and sunglasses) and play a particular blend of hard-edged progressive bluegrass that emphasizes a rock stance and expressivity more than instrumental virtuosity. The band still records popular retextings of American songs by Bohouš Chaloupek (who long ago emigrated to the United States), for example, "Harley" ("White Freightliner Blues"), "Myslím na Colorado" (I'm thinking of Colorado), and "Tennessee Waltz"—all of which appear on this record. Chaloupek's versions of these and many other songs are widely known in bluegrass circles, and are widely played in Czech jams. Cop is still appreciated by older crowds, but their approach appeals less to younger audiences, who don't connect with this group's recycling of older material and tropes.

Druhá Tráva. *Best and Last*. Venkow/Universal 1539332, 2001. 2 compact discs.

This compilation includes a selection of recordings by the group Druhá Tráva, whose name can be translated as either "Second Grass" or "Other Grass," both of which suit this ensemble, which started close to bluegrass but has shifted to highlight the instrumental and ensemble virtuosity of the members, and the poetic lyrics and delivery of frontman Robert Křesťan. This collection includes seminal works that speak to the group's founding during the transition of the early 1990s—and to Křesťan's lyrical gift. The early song "Praha bolestivosti" (Threshold of pain) plays with the words *Praha* (Prague) and *práh* (threshold) in highlighting the role of the Czech capital in the 1989 "Velvet Revolution" and the unsettled times that it brought, using a poetic treatment of human relations to provide social commentary, a pattern that is also visible in "Panenka" (Maiden), a song Křesťan wrote while part of the Brno-based group Poutníci (Pilgrims) during the 1980s.

Druhá Tráva. *Shuttle to Bethlehem*. Indies Happy Trails MAM659-2, 2011. Compact disc.

This collection of songs by Robert Křesťan translated into English was intended for the US market. Druhá Tráva has toured the United States consistently since the mid-1990s, so while most of their records are sung primarily in Czech, with a song or two in English, they occasionally release an album sung primarily in English. Writer and journalist Ruth Ellen Gruber carried out the translations, in collaboration with Robert; she speaks about this process in the film *Banjo Romantika*.

Greenhorns. *Zlatá éra 1967–1974* (The golden era, 1967–1974). Supraphon 5802-2, 2007. 3 compact discs.

This collection features many of the band's early hits, showing the range of songs that the group retexted and translated, from the lush exoticism of "El Paso" to the plaintive landscape painting of "Red River Valley." In this period, the Greenhorns (Zelenáči) were joined by Michal Tučný, a powerful singer with a clear, high voice. His smooth delivery on songs like "Vlak půlnoční" (their retexting of "I'm So Lonesome I Could Cry") contrasts with the singing of Jan Vyčítal and Josef Šimek, who match Johnny Cash on songs like "Když náš táta hrál" ("When Papa Played the Dobro") and "Oranžový expres" ("Orange Blossom Special").

Křesťan, Robert, and Druhá Tráva. *Dylanovky*. Universal 174 428-9, 2007.

The title of this album is not readily translatable—it is a way of saying "songs by Dylan," using the *-ovka* suffix (pl.*-ovky*) that I have heard used in bluegrass circles as a way to refer to songs linked to a certain author or performer. For instance, gospel songs known to be associated with bandleader Doyle Lawson are sometimes identified using his band's name, Quicksilver: *Quicksilverovka*. Robert Křesťan's "day job" is creating literary translations of modern English-language literature for Czech readers, so this concept album is a logical variant on the longstanding Czech practice of retexting American songs. The band's sound strays quite far from bluegrass on this record, including elements of Irish traditional music, jazz, and rock. For example, while Luboš Malina's banjo is still prominent in "Señore," their version of Dylan's "Señor (Tales of Yankee Power)," hard-driving drum beats and electric guitar licks compete with him for acoustic space in the mix.

Kůs, Petr, and Fámy. *Fámy* (Rumors). Petr Kůs, 1999. Compact disc.

Petr Kůs is a Prague native, a teacher by profession, but also a mandolinist, bandleader, and songwriter who has worked with the influential bands Blanket, Quartet, and Vabank Unit, and as of 2017 leads the band Fámy. Kůs is known as a skilled songwriter, but one particular comment I have heard about him (made by other Czech bluegrassers) is that his Czech texts "feel" like American (English) texts. Kůs's website pokes fun at his reputation for writing in Czech with an American feel, joking that his hit song "Zlatá rybka" (The golden fish) is "actually by Bob Dylan" (http://www.famy.cz/#O%20N%C3%81S, accessed April 7, 2017).

Kůs, Petr. *Nezralé mládí* (Immature youth). Good Day Records, 2006. Compact disc.

This release by Kůs features Dutch guitarist Ralph Schut, as well as a full slate of original compositions with Kůs's trademark smooth, technically polished sound. With "Když se tak dívám výš" (When I look up higher) he continues his history of retexting and creating songs that evoke a gospel feel without including a hard-hitting religious message. "Bejby, buď mou" (Baby, be mine) is an example of his more upbeat side, with a bluesy bounce that also carries the title track.

Liška-Malina-Nejtek. *Fragile Bliss*. Animal Music 053-2, 2015. Compact disc.

Banjoist Luboš Malina has worked on a number of side projects outside of his role as bandleader for Druhá Tráva, recording his own exploratory albums as well as playing with singer Kateřina Garcia (a mix of Spanish and Celtic material) and the group Kon Sira (Sephardic songs). This album uses a jazz framework to continue this exploration of style, sound, and technique, featuring Malina's banjo and an array of whistles and other wind instruments along with the more straight-ahead jazz approach of Tomaš Liška (bass) and Michal Nejtek (piano).

Malina Brothers. *Rychlejší koně* ("Faster Horses"). Pepa Malina, 2013. Compact disc.

This family band, composed of Luboš Malina (banjo and whistles), his brother Pavel (guitar), and their half-brother Josef "Pepa" (fiddle), is a side project for these professionals, all of whom have multiple other work roles. The record's eclectic mix of material reflects their personal and family histories, and a sense that the three of them are reflecting on their pasts. It includes Czech-texted Americana such as the title track, as well as a wistful version of "Lady Yesterday" and a romp through "Skočná," a dance taken from Czech composer Bedřich Smetana's opera *The Bartered Bride*, a tune that Luboš recorded with the Brno band Poutníci in the 1980s. The group has developed from a side project to a lasting part of the brothers' work, with a release in 2015 in collaboration with Nashville veteran Charlie McCoy, and a US tour in 2016.

Monogram. *Siesta*. Monogram, 2000. Compact disc.

In 2016 Monogram celebrated their twenty-fifth year as a band (with some changes in personnel along the way). Founded by the Jahoda brothers, Jaromír (banjo) and Zdeněk (mandolin), the group in 2000 included guitarist and singer Jakub Racek. This album, produced by Slavek Hanzlík, an acclaimed Czech guitarist and an émigré to the United States, includes original songs by Racek and instrumentals by the Jahodas, as well as "Gone" by European bluegrass booster Liz Meyer. Racek does a spot-on performance of James Taylor's "Fire and Rain" in which almost no trace of vocal accent can be heard, a rare thing in any Czech performance.

Reliéf. *Leaves in the Wind.* Good Day Records, 1999. Compact disc.

Reliéf were quite a young band in the late 1990s when they began attracting attention on the Czech scene with their idiomatic singing, tight harmonies, and skillful instrumental work. Bandleader, banjoist, dobroist, and songwriter Zbyněk Bureš is a polymath who ties together the substantial abilities of the group and makes them more than the sum of their parts. One measure of Zbyněk's songwriting ability is that an original gospel song he wrote, "The Lord Will Answer Thee," was recorded by one of the most prominent gospel groups in bluegrass, Doyle Lawson and Quicksilver, on the album *Winding through Life* (Sugar Hill, 1999).

Reliéf. *Suburban Street.* Good Day Records, 2003. Compact disc.

Composed mostly of original songs by Zbyněk Bureš, along with covers of "Cold, Cold Ground" and Tom Waits's "Wait 'til Yesterday Is Here," this collection shows how the group and Zbyněk's songwriting have shifted away from a more traditionalist take on bluegrass, and from gospel material. The bluegrass numbers are strong, but the most powerful number in my opinion is the achingly forlorn country lament "Poor Country."

Reliéf. *Live.* Good Day Records, 2006. Compact disc.

The release of this tour-de-force performance in Prague's Palmovka Theater includes twenty songs. This sampling of the group's repertoire reflects their increasingly cerebral choice of material—due in large part to Zbyněk Bureš, who wrote most of them, with the exception of their cover of Bob Dylan's "Señor (Tales of Yankee Power)." A highlight is their rendition of "Už větry tichnou" (Already the breezes are quieting), a parody of early twentieth-century tramp song, which they took from the repertoire of the group Bobři (Beavers). There are only two sacred numbers on this record, "Go Right Out" and "There Is a God."

Reliéf. *That's Not for You.* Good Day Records, 2011. Compact disc.

This is the final recording (as of this writing in 2017) by the band. It includes no gospel numbers, and while there are some in-the-pocket bluegrass sounds ("Dear Shelly," for example), the majority of the selections are less tied to that style. While they all stick to bluegrass-type instrumentation and textures, songs like "Alone with the Blues" and "Of Course Him" depart markedly from bluegrass techniques and narrative approach.

Roh, Zdeněk, and Guests, with Roll's Boys. *Raising the Bar*. Roll's Productions, 2008. Compact disc.

In this project, Zdeněk alternates between a number of sounds to encompass his expansive interests and abilities. The record presents the country-influenced bluegrass sounds of the band Roll's Boys playing a mix of covers and original material (like the first track, "When the Grasses Grow So Well"), and an ensemble with electric guitar and pedal steel (played by Zbyněk Bureš in a guest appearance) that mixes country sounds with more stylistically adventurous material like "Vanished Footsteps" and "Man at the Old Playground." The cover of "He's Got You" (a transformation of the classic "She's Got You") is a particularly strong example of smoothly aggressive "mash" bluegrass.

Seeger, Pete. *Pete Seeger in Prague, 1964*. Flyright 68 and 69, 2002. 2 compact discs.

This release features a recording of Seeger's famous 1964 concert in Prague made by Gene Deitch, a US-born animator and artist who had moved to the Czech Republic to live in the late 1950s. The package from the British Flyright label includes recordings that Seeger made especially for Deitch, with explanatory narration about the history of the texts, melodies, and instruments. Deitch and Seeger were longtime friends, and Seeger sent Deitch a recording of recollections of his Prague visit in 1964 that is also included.

Sunny Side. *Staří Greenhorni*. Self-produced, 2001. Compact disc.

This release by Sunny Side is atypical in that it is sung all in Czech. The group usually sings (almost religiously) in English, preferring a traditionalist approach to bluegrass that extends to their choice of ties, suits, and headwear. In this tribute to the Greenhorns, the band underscores the influence that Marko Čermák and his bandmates have had on the Czech music scene, and on generations of bluegrassers. Frontman Pavel Handlík's clear tenor soars convincingly through songs that were originally recorded by the Greenhorns' Michal Tučný, finding its mark especially on numbers like "Vlak půlnoční" (Midnight Train) and "Řekněte jí" (Tell her).

Taxmeni. *The Best Of*. Venkow/Universal 0144032, 2001. 2 compact discs.

Taxmeni, founded in 1970, represent a stream of musical Americanism called Česká Country (Czech country), which is the core of the material played on Prague's Country Radio station, 89.5 FM (www.countryradio.cz), and thus is heard in many working-class contexts such as workplaces and intercity buses. This collection includes retextings of musical Americana, including "Dědečkovy hodiny," the group's version of the Henry Clay Work song and bluegrass classic "My Grandfather's Clock," as well as "Hledaný muž," which is a version of the song "Wanted Man," co-written by Bob Dylan and Johnny Cash.

Teagrass. *Večírek* (Party). Indies Records MAM176-2, 2002. Compact disc.

Headed by musician, chemist, and music producer Jiří Plocek, Teagrass mixes the styles that are listed on this CD's package: "World Music, East European Folk Music, Bluegrass, Swing, Klezmer." Such an approach is rare; most groups try either to approximate American sounds or to continue established forms of Czech country or bluegrass. This release is a live recording made in Brno's Stará Pekárna (Old Bakery) club, and it sizzles with energy throughout. Guest appearances by Kateřina Garcia and Luboš Malina bring both folkloric and cosmopolitan sounds that complement Plocek's distinctive mandolin and fiddler Stanislav "Stano" Palúch's command of jazz and folkloric styles.

Trampské Písně 1920–1939. Supraphon 5379-2301, 2002. Compact disc.

This collection of tramp songs (most recorded in Berlin) features performers who were popularizing this form on vaudeville and theater stages in Czechoslovakia in the era of the interwar First Republic. The exuberance of the singers is palpable, with sparkling close-harmony vocals on fast-paced songs like "Chata v lese" (Cabin in the woods) by Settleři (the Settlers) and unabashed sentimentality on the tramp anthem "Vlajka" (Flag).

Films

Balada pro banditu (Ballad for a bandit). Directed by Vladimír Sís, 1978.

This film dramatizes Ivan Olbracht's 1933 novel *Nikola Šuhaj loupežník* (Nikola Šuhaj the robber), setting it both in the Ruthenian mountains of Olbracht's story and at a Czechoslovak tramping gathering, complete with campfire, guitars, military backpacks, and cowboy hats. The songs by composer Miloš Štědroň further the in-betweenness by referencing at times Central European folklore, tramp songs, and Czech country; the soundtrack is dominated instrumentally by the Greenhorns, including banjoist Marko Čermák.

Banjo Romantika. Directed by Shara Lange. Produced by Lee Bidgood and Shara K. Lange, 2015.

This feature-length documentary film is based on the research in this volume, and includes many of the musicians and places described in these pages. It is available through Documentary Educational Resources, http://www.der.org/films/banjo-romantika.html.

Big Picture: The Story of American Forces Network (AFN). Army Pictorial Center, 1962.

This film details the workings of US military media outlets in France and Germany in the early 1960s, providing footage of the *Stickbuddy Jamboree*, a country music show that broadcast from AFN Munich and was heard by many Czechs, including banjoist Marko Čermák. It is available in high-quality form from the National Archives and Records Administration, but is more accessible online at https://archive.org/details/gov.archives.arc.2569813.

Limonadový Joe aneb Koňská opera (Lemonade Joe, or the Horse Opera). Directed by Oldřich Lipský. Filmové studio Barrandov, 1964.

Even as this parody of American western films pokes fun at both capitalism and the film genre, it shows a great love for the image of the cowboy that it lampoons. While it doesn't feature any concrete traces of bluegrass, it includes a number of musical Americanisms, including a New Orleans–style funeral march and the quasi-English song "Sou fár tu jú aj mej," which translates—or perhaps transliterates—as "So far to you I may."

Tramping in Bohemia. Produced by Margot Buff, 2011.

This short documentary follows a group of aging Czechs as they retrace steps that they took as youths riding the trains and hiking the woods, visiting storied tramping sites—and singing many songs along the way. In addition to providing background information on the current Czech tramping movement, the film conveys a sense of how tramps continue their activities in the present. It is not available commercially, but can be viewed on the filmmaker's website, http://www.margotbuff.com/tramping-in-bohemia/.

Websites

http://bacr.cz

The official website of the Bluegrassová asociace Ceské republiky (Bluegrass association of the Czech Republic) provides a listing of bands, festivals, concerts, and other information, as well as archives of their quarterly publication *Bluegrassové listy*, and a more exhaustive discography of Czech bluegrass releases (listed under the link Česká CD). It offers an English version.

https://www.banjolit.com/music/

Slovak banjoist and entrepreneur Richard Ciferský offers a number of items and services on his Banjolit website: innovative accessories for musicians (particularly banjoists), as well as his services as an event producer and promoter—including for foreign artists who would like to tour in Europe.

http://bgcz.net

A social networking site, BlueGrassCZ offers a number of services, primary among which are the discussion forums, which include classified ads that host a brisk trade in bluegrass-related instruments. The vast majority of the activity on this site is in Czech.

INDEX

LEE BIDGOOD is an associate professor of bluegrass, old-time, and country music studies in the Department of Appalachian Studies at East Tennessee State University.

FOLKLORE STUDIES IN A MULTICULTURAL WORLD

The Amazing Crawfish Boat
John Laudun
(University Press of Mississippi)

Building New Banjos for an Old-Time World
Richard Jones-Bamman
(University of Illinois Press)

City of Neighborhoods: Memory, Folklore, and Ethnic Place in Boston
Anthony Bak Buccitelli
(University of Wisconsin Press)

Czech Bluegrass: Notes from the Heart of Europe
Lee Bidgood
(University of Illinois Press)

Daisy Turner's Kin: An African American Family Saga
Jane C. Beck
(University of Illinois Press)

Global Tarantella: Reinventing Southern Italian Folk Music and Dances
Incoronata Inserra
(University of Illinois Press)

If You Don't Laugh You'll Cry: The Occupational Humor of White Wisconsin Prison Workers
Claire Schmidt
(University of Wisconsin Press)

Improvised Adolescence: Somali Bantu Teenage Refugees in America
Sandra Grady
(University of Wisconsin Press)

The Jumbies' Playing Ground: Old World Influence on Afro-Creole Masquerades in the Eastern Caribbean
Robert Wyndham Nicholls
(University Press of Mississippi)

The Last Laugh: Folk Humor, Celebrity Culture, and Mass-Mediated Disasters in the Digital Age
Trevor J. Blank
(University of Wisconsin Press)

The Painted Screens of Baltimore: An Urban Folk Art Revealed
Elaine Eff
(University Press of Mississippi)

Recasting Folk in the Himalayas: Indian Music, Media, and Social Mobility
Stefan Fiol
(University of Illinois Press)

Squeeze This! A Cultural History of the Accordion in American
Marion Jacobson
(University of Illinois Press)
Stable Views: Stories and Voices from the Thoroughbred Racetrack
Ellen E. McHale
(University Press of Mississippi)
Storytelling in Siberia: The Olonkho Epic in a Changing World
Robin P. Harris
(University of Illinois Press)
Ukrainian Otherlands: Diaspora, Homeland, and Folk Imagination in the Twentieth Century
Natalia Khanenko-Friesen
(University Press of Mississippi)
A Vulgar Art: A New Approach to Stand-Up Comedy
Ian Brodie
(University Press of Mississippi)

The University of Illinois Press
is a founding member of the
Association of American University Presses.

Composed in 10.25/13 Minion Pro
with Myriad Pro display
by Kirsten Dennison
at the University of Illinois Press
Cover designed by Jason Gabbert
Cover illustration: Nadezda Murmakova/Shutterstock.com

University of Illinois Press
1325 South Oak Street
Champaign, IL 61820-6903
www.press.uillinois.edu